The
Light
and Fast
Organisation

The
Light
and Fast
Organisation

A New Way of Dealing with **Uncertainty**

Patrick Hollingworth

WILEY

First published in 2016 by John Wiley & Sons Australia, Ltd
42 McDougall St, Milton Qld 4064
Office also in Melbourne

Typeset in 11/15 pt Avenir LT Std by Aptara, India

© The Trustee for the Patrick Hollingworth Family Trust 2016

The moral rights of the author have been asserted

National Library of Australia Cataloguing-in-Publication data:

Creator:	Hollingworth, Patrick, author.
Title:	The Light and Fast Organisation: A new way of dealing with uncertainty / Patrick Hollingworth.
ISBN:	9780730328278 (pbk.)
	9780730328285 (ebook)
Notes:	Includes index.
Subjects:	Organizational change—Management.
	Leadership.
	Management.
	Success in business.
Dewey Number:	658.406

Cover design by Wiley

Cover and internal climber images by Sam Scopelliti and Patrick Hollingworth

by C.O.S. Printers Pte Ltd

10 9 8 7 6 5 4 3 2 1

Disclaimer
The material in this publication is of the nature of general comment only, and does not represent professional advice. It is not intended to provide specific guidance for particular circumstances and it should not be relied on as the basis for any decision to take action or not take action on any matter which it covers. Readers should obtain professional advice where appropriate, before making any such decision. To the maximum extent permitted by law, the author and publisher disclaim all responsibility and liability to any person, arising directly or indirectly from any person taking or not taking action based on the information in this publication.

Contents

About the author

Patrick Hollingworth works with people, teams and organisations to help them deal with a world which is becoming more volatile, uncertain, complex and ambiguous by the day.

After studying anthropology, geography and psychology at university, he spent a decade with a large international consultancy, working on some of the largest and most complex infrastructure projects ever built in Australia. He's seen the very best of what large organisations can create, and also the very worst.

At the same time he began exploring the uncertainty and complexity which go hand in hand with mountaineering, learning the art of alpine style in the mountains of New Zealand, Canada and France, and then the science of expedition style in the mountains of Alaska, Argentina, Nepal, Pakistan and Tibet.

It's taken him to great heights — literally. He's summited multiple 8000 metre peaks, including Mount Everest, and over the past 15 years has been a member of small *light* and *fast* alpine-style teams and has led rather large *heavy* and *slow* expedition-style teams. He's seen the very best of what alpine style can offer, and also the very worst of what expedition style can deliver.

Patrick *lives* and *breathes* this stuff.

He is based in Australia and travels internationally to deliver keynote presentations, workshops, mentoring and consulting to a range of organisations. These include multinational companies such as British retailer Marks and Spencer, American energy giant Chevron and British-Australian mining company Rio Tinto, through to mid-sized, Australian, Asian and European banks, medical and technology companies, and government departments and educational institutions.

Find out more at **www.patrickhollingworth.com**

Introduction

There is a mountain face in Switzerland that from 1933 to 1938 held the attention of the world. Not just the attention of the mountaineering world, but the *entire* world. A mountain face so steep and imposing that it had become legend: one that, at last count, has killed at least 64 people who have attempted to climb it.

Extending in an unbroken upward thrust for nearly 2 kilometres, this vertical and overhanging face comprised of mixed rock and ice has variously been described as 'ferociously steep', 'inaccessible', 'unclimbable' and 'murderous'. Known as the Nordwand, German for 'North Face', it belongs to the 3970-metre-high mountain called the Eiger.

Located in the Bernese Oberland in the northernmost portion of the Alps, the Eiger acts as a weather beacon and attracts the earliest of bad weather moving down from the northern plains of Europe. Not only is the Eiger's North Face incredibly high and steep, it is also somewhat concave, giving it a tendency to collect and amplify storms as they hit. Sunny days and warm temperatures can turn to maelstrom and freezing conditions within minutes, creating blizzards, deadly rockfalls and avalanches. The normal rules for mountain weather just don't seem to apply here.

The Nordwand is a powerful metaphor for the world we are living in today.

At this critical juncture in our history, we too are experiencing unpredictable and violent storms. Fuelled by never before seen and ever more complex interactions between people, places and technology, the sunny days and warm weather of the past are gone and we are now seemingly inundated with maelstrom, freezing conditions, blizzards, rockfalls and avalanches. For most people and most organisations—those that don't have the mindset and skills required to deal with this volatility and uncertainty—it's a terrifying and stressful place to be. It is inherently uncomfortable.

But for the few people and organisations that do have the right mindset and skills, it's actually an incredibly exciting time. There is immeasurable opportunity, unlike any other period in the history of mankind. The purpose of this book is to arm you, the reader, with the right mindset and skills to ensure that you, and the organisation you work for, can experience the excitement and take advantage of the opportunities ahead.

To understand more about the right mindset and skills needed to take advantage of these opportunities, in this book we are going to delve into the world of the mountaineer, a place not commonly associated with meaningful learning beyond superficial colloquialisms about 'dreaming big', 'never giving up' and 'anything is possible if you try hard enough'.

More specifically, we are going into the world of a subset of mountaineers who climb *light* and *fast*, an approach known as *alpine style*. (We call this type of mountaineer the *alpinist*.)

There is arguably no type of person on earth who has a better understanding of the skills, knowledge and mindset needed to deal with the type of volatility, uncertainty, complexity and ambiguity that the world is enshrouded in today. And so, throughout this book, we are going to learn from the alpinist.

But just for a moment, we must go back to Switzerland in 1935.

Standing above the beautiful alpine meadows of the tourist resorts of Kleine Scheidegg and Grindelwald, in the 1930s the North Face of the Eiger became a global stage against which a group of young German and Austrian men pitted their lives in a tragic fashion. Although the mountain had previously been climbed via comparatively easier routes such as the south and the Mittellegi ridges, no-one had ever climbed directly up the North Face.

For the young men involved, each seemingly oblivious to their soon-to-be starring roles on the world stage, their motivation to climb the North Face was the intrinsic joy and challenge that mountaineering provides. But Hitler's Third Reich seized upon their feats as an opportunity to showcase the talent and supposed superiority of their citizens to the world. (It was even reported that following the Munich Olympics Adolf Hitler offered gold medals to any German or Austrian climbers who could successfully scale the face). And so during the mid 1930s, as Europe slowly lumbered towards another world war, the global spotlight was centred very much on the Eiger's main stage, the North Face.

The first serious attempt occurred in the summer of 1935, when two young Bavarians named Max Sedlmayr and Karl Mehringer set up camp in the meadows below the face. With youthful exuberance on their side and the best equipment available at the time, they were as ready as could be for the challenge above them. Regarded as quiet but very experienced and hardened climbers, the pair spent a number of weeks reconnoitring the lower part of the route before launching their final upward assault on the face under clear blue skies very early in the morning of Wednesday 21 August.

As crowds gathered throughout the day to watch via telescopes the pair's progress from Kleine Scheidegg and Grindelwald, Sedlmayr and Mehringer made rapid upwards progress. By the time the last of the summer twilight was fading in the west, they had climbed the easier lower third of the face and were looking likely to succeed: perhaps two more days on the face and they would have it in the bag. Thursday morning dawned clear and the pair recommenced their upward push.

However, the increasingly difficult terrain of mixed rock and ice slowed their progress considerably. Whereas on the first day they had climbed 900 vertical metres, by the end of the second day they had only covered a further 300 vertical metres. Although the gallery of spectators in Kleine Scheidegg and Grindelwald had been initially confident of the pair's success, by the end of the second day many were questioning whether they had any chance before the next storm arrived. And rightly so. The Friday morning brought with it thick mist and fog, an eerie calm before the storm, and by the end of that day neither Sedlmayr nor Mehringer had been sighted on the face for some hours.

On Friday night, the calm weather finally broke and all of Saturday and Sunday a fierce storm lashed the mountain with thunder and lightning, strong winds and snow. The night-time temperatures in Kleine Scheidegg dropped to −8 degrees Celsius — how cold must it have been up on the face? During a short period of respite on Sunday afternoon the storm backed off and afforded the spectators in the valley the briefest of views of the face, where they momentarily saw Sedlmayr and Mehringer bravely battling onwards and upwards. This was quite remarkable, especially after five bitterly cold days and four nights on the face. But the reality was that Sedlmayr and Mehringer had climbed themselves into a trap: the icy conditions had frozen both the rock and their ropes, making descent impossible. Soon enough the clouds closed in again, and the pair were never seen alive again.

Numerous searches were conducted in the days and weeks following their disappearance, but no trace of the men could be found. It was only on 19 September, nearly a month after they had been last seen, that a search plane piloted by a famous German flying ace passing extremely close to the face spotted the body of one of the men, knee-deep in the snow and frozen standing upright, still a long way beneath the summit. The North Face had claimed its first human lives.

The following summer saw a second serious attempt on the face, made this time by a young but skilled four-man party comprising two Germans and two Austrians, seemingly unperturbed by the previous year's events. If the expedition of 1935 was a tragedy, the events of 1936 were truly macabre.

After four days the team had made excellent progress up the first two-thirds of the face, but they were forced into a sudden retreat when a rockfall caused a head injury to one of the team members.

Over the ensuing 24 hours, and in a worsening storm, the four climbers progressively succumbed to the elements, with the last climber literally freezing to death and whispering his infamous final words, *I'm finished*, within an arm's reach of the rescue party. These events are to this day considered to be among the greatest mountaineering tragedies ever documented.

It was in the summer of 1938 that success on the North Face of the Eiger was finally achieved. Again, a team of four young men comprising two Germans and two Austrians tackled the face, and after four days of considerable hard work and suffering, accompanied by the requisite storms, rockfalls and avalanches and stories of near death, the party stood atop the narrow summit. The celebrations were, however, all too brief, as before long the fog of World War II descended on Europe and feats of daring on the great mountain were relegated to history.

Over the ensuing decades, more attempts were made on the face, some successful and many unsuccessful. Many more climbers lost their lives. But the world had moved on. No longer did an ascent of the world's most dangerous mountain face garner the attention of the global spotlight. Not, that is, until 2008.

Switzerland, February 2008

Early on the morning of Wednesday 13 February, leading Swiss alpinist Ueli Steck took the short train ride from his lakeside home town of Interlaken up to the small ski resort at Kleine Scheidegg at the foot of the Eiger. Most of the people on the train would have been dressed in thick, warm clothing, ready for a day of skiing: some light-hearted recreation, and nothing more. Indeed, Steck probably looked inconspicuous: rather than thick clothing and skis, he wore only lightweight attire and carried with him a tiny backpack, a thin climbing rope and a pair of short technical ice axes. Few, if any, people on the train that morning were aware of what Steck was about to do.

Less than three hours later Steck was standing on the summit of the Eiger, having completely rewritten the mountaineering record books and in doing so creating a new genre of mountaineering known as *extreme alpinism*. Steck made history that morning by climbing the North Face in record time, dramatically changing perceptions around what is possible when a commitment to climbing *light* and *fast* is made. What had taken the first ascensionists in 1938 four days — or 96 hours — to complete, Steck had finished in a staggering time of only 2 hours, 47 minutes and 33 seconds.

The sport of mountaineering would never be the same again.

How did he do it?

How did Steck achieve such an incredible feat?

On the surface, Steck's approach was staggeringly simple: he climbed light and he climbed fast.

Steck chose to solo the route *fast*, meaning he climbed without a climbing partner or team members. This enabled him to climb the entire face unroped (although he did carry a lightweight rope just in case), meaning he did not have to spend time belaying other climbers up each pitch. The benefits of this approach then greatly amplified his ability to travel *light*: the time he saved meant he was able to climb the entire face in one day, removing the need for heavy overnight bivvy equipment such as a sleeping bag, mattress and gas stove. As a result, Steck's pack was incredibly light. Steck was himself also extremely light. In preparation for this attempt he had trained particularly hard, with his aim being to strip all unnecessary fat and muscle from his body to improve his power-to-weight ratio. Renowned as a highly disciplined trainer, he shed nearly 10 kilograms in preparation for the climb, which was approximately 15 per cent of his body weight.

Steck also flipped the wider climbing community's prevailing beliefs about the best time of year to climb the Eiger. Most parties attempted the route in summer, when the face is relatively free of snow and ice. Steck on the other hand had chosen to climb the face during winter, when it was completely iced up. The benefit to this approach was that by using ice axes and crampons for the entire duration of the climb, he could skirt across the frozen winter ice much more quickly than he could if the rock were dry. In addition, the risk of rockfalls was significantly reduced as the rocks freeze in place during winter.

Describing his speed climb of the North Face, he said (with a rich Swiss accent):

> You reach the point where you are into it…As fast as possible to the summit…your hands, your ice axe and your crampons, and they have to just move…You're progressing…that's what it's all about. You want to keep moving, having progress in your life.

Belying the apparent simplicity of his approach, underneath the surface was a very complex web of prior experience from which Steck was able to draw in order to achieve his record time. Steck was no one-hit wonder: he had begun climbing at an early age and by the time he was 18 he had already climbed the North Face of the Eiger as part of a team of four, an incredible feat in itself. By the mid 2000s Steck had built up an extensive résumé of difficult climbs in the European Alps, the Alaska Range and the Himalaya.

Starting out as a rock climber, he progressed towards technical mountaineering and then high-altitude mountaineering, before starting to further refine his specialty to fast solo ascents, initially on the relatively lower mountains of the Alps (such as the Eiger), before taking this approach to the ultimate mountaineering testing ground of the Himalaya. (In 2011 he soloed the south face of Shishapangma, an 8000-metre mountain in Tibet, in a record time of 10.5 hours, and in 2013 he soloed the south face of 8091-metre Annapurna, the world's tenth highest mountain, in a record time of 28 hours; it takes most parties at least one week to reach the summit after *months* of acclimatising).

In his book *Outliers* journalist Malcolm Gladwell popularised the work of Dr Anders Ericsson, a Swedish psychologist whose research revealed that natural ability requires ten years, or 10000 hours of practice, to be made manifest. Steck is the perfect example of the '10000 hours rule', his lifetime spent in the mountains in preparation for the day that he could turn the sport of mountaineering on its head.

And that's what he did on that clear blue day in February 2008.

What can we learn?

So what does all of this mean? It's an inspiring story, yes, but what else can we make of this? What relevance does this story have for us all?

As described earlier, the North Face of the Eiger can be a metaphor for the world in which we are living today, complete with storms, rockfalls and avalanches, and we have no choice but to climb it.

The concave nature of the North Face serves to amplify the magnitude of the storms that strike her. Similarly, the interconnectedness of our world today serves to amplify the storms that strike us, and, as you will read in the following pages, there is a perfect storm of a magnitude never before seen that is just starting to reach us.

The purpose of this book is to provide a manifesto for improving the way in which you and the organisation you work for can adapt to the changes and challenges facing us all. This has been tested and proved in the alpine world, and now you can use it as the storm descends around us.

Regardless of the forthcoming storm, we have a choice as to how we tackle the climb ahead.

We can choose to continue to do things like we have always done, and climb the face in a traditional manner (it's called *expedition style*, it's *heavy* and *slow*, and we'll learn more about it later). We *may* still get to the top, but it will take us a long time, and we probably won't survive the storm.

Or, we can choose to flip conventional thinking on its head and, following Steck's lead, take a new approach and climb *light* and *fast* to help us get through the maelstrom. If we do choose to take this approach (and to be honest, we don't have any other option), there will be difficult times ahead, complete with much discomfort and doubt. We will have to face our fears.

So let us get to work. Onward and upward we must go!

PART I

The landscape

We are again immigrants in time, as our perfect storm is reshaping society, business and institutional thinking.

CHAPTER 1

The perfect storm?

In this chapter, we'll try to understand change through:
- **the VUCA framework**
- **the three factors of people, places and technology that can combine to create the perfect storm**
- **the three-stage framework.**

In his classic nonfiction book *The Perfect Storm*, Sebastian Junger tells the story of the fishing boat the *Andrea Gail* and her crew. Lost at sea in 1991, they were caught off the northeast coast of the USA in a super-storm created by an incredibly rare combination of three weather systems. At its peak, the storm had wind strengths in excess of 120 kilometres per hour, and it generated some of the largest waves ever recorded.

Few people took the weather warnings from the National Weather Service seriously. It was only once the true magnitude of the storm became apparent that people started reacting, with thousands along the eastern seaboard evacuating their homes.

Other than a few small pieces of debris, no trace of the Andrea Gail *or her six crewmen was ever found.*

This 'perfect storm' killed another seven people and created widespread destruction on much of the eastern coastline, causing an estimated damage bill of $200 million.

It may seem strange to call something so destructive *perfect* but, in weather terms, this combination of conditions is so rare it has to be seen as miraculous. Sure, two weather systems occasionally merge together to create powerful storms, but *three* systems merging together? It was unprecedented. Negativity does not necessarily diminish perfection.

The three forces

Today a similar perfect storm, albeit a metaphorical one, is brewing. Just like the real perfect storm that took the *Andrea Gail* and her crew to a watery grave, a never-before-seen combination of three forces is occurring to create a perfect storm, the likes of which the world has never seen before.

What are these three forces? We will get to them in a minute. But first, it is crucial to understand that the impact of this perfect storm will be felt all over the globe. The old world of business will never be the same again.

Instead, the storm is giving birth to a new world order.

Speaking about the post–World War II era, cultural anthropologist Margaret Mead once wrote, 'All of us who grew up before the war are immigrants in time, immigrants from an earlier world, living in an age essentially different from anything we knew before'. We are again immigrants in time, as our perfect storm is reshaping society, business and institutional thinking.

Everything from how we play and how we learn to how we work and how we govern — in other words, how we live our lives — is being profoundly changed.

The three forces that have combined to form this perfect storm are:

1.   people
2.   places
3.   technology.

The capacity for *people* to connect with one another to communicate, share, learn and trade is increasing quickly and easily. This is happening in both virtual and real *places* through *technology*'s rapid growth.

What does this mean?

It means the world has become flatter, more transparent and more accessible than ever before. It also means that there are more opportunities for cultural misunderstanding, misalignment and clashes that would not have happened when isolation was more prevalent. And it means that many of the organisations that supply society's daily needs are in danger of disruption and failure. We are seeing increasing evidence of this misunderstanding and misalignment of cultures, and the disruptive impacts on business, on a daily basis.

So when did this perfect storm start?

It's been brewing for quite some time, but the signals were too weak for our business and societal radars to pick up. 9/11 is a perfect example of what we thought of as an isolated incident; but then came the Bali Bombings, followed by similar events in Madrid, London, Mumbai and Paris. The Global Financial Crisis (GFC) of 2008 seemed like a once-in-a-century financial crash — and yet nearly a decade later we are still dealing with its fallout, and talk of another, even larger, debt-caused crisis persists.

These events all involved *people*, *places* and *technology* rapidly moving together to create a sense of unease and urgency, sending us racing for metaphorical cover.

Like thunderclouds, these events were early indicators of the approaching perfect storm.

Storm outriders

In the mountains, we call early indicators of unrest *storm outriders*. Days before any other sign of approaching weather, clear blue skies gradually become streaked with thin, wispy strands of white or grey cirrus cloud, which are formed by very strong winds blowing up high. Those of us who have been around the mountains for long enough know these storm outriders are a sign of things to come: the weather will start deteriorating within the next 24 to 48 hours.

Simply put, they are a warning:

Get off the mountain, and get off fast, or the weather will take its own measures to remove you.

What we are seeing now across the globe are storm outriders. Strong winds of change are starting to blow our way, and events—which may at first seem disjointed and disparate—are starting to show connections involving these three key forces of people, places and technology. This perfect storm is about to try to take us off the mountain by whatever means.

And, just like Cyclone Tracy and Hurricane Katrina and Typhoon Haiyan, this storm's got a name. It's called *VUCA* (pronounced voo-ka).

VUCA

VUCA stands for:

- volatility
- uncertainty
- complexity
- ambiguity.

It is perhaps *the* best acronym that encapsulates the impact this perfect storm is starting to unleash upon the globe.

The acronym has its origins in the US military. Devised as a description of the post–Cold War landscape and first referenced in print in 1991, its use became more frequent in the military post-9/11, particularly at military academies, as a way of articulating to young officer candidates the new world in which the US military would be operating. (The US military has several other acronyms that are perhaps equally applicable to our situation, but they are less polite and probably shouldn't feature in this book.)

The VUCA acronym may be military in origin, but it is becoming increasingly relevant to business and broader society as we get closer to the full impact of the perfect storm.

But beyond its status in the popular business vernacular, what does it actually mean?

VUCA describes the *nature* of the change that the world is currently facing: its parameters describe how change *will* affect us on a daily basis. We can already see it happening; the business landscape is becoming more volatile and uncertain. It is more ambiguous, especially as the rate of technological innovation increases day by day. This technological innovation is leading to increased interconnectedness across the globe, which is in turn resulting in increased complexity.

VUCA is change

In a phenomenon known as *change fatigue*, we've all become a bit jaded when it comes to 'change', especially at work. Organisational change. Change management. Change management consultants. Yawn.

We've all experienced 'change initiatives' in the workplace before, but let me ask you something: when you've completed the 'initiative', have you felt that any *meaningful* change has actually been initiated?

Even one of the world's leading experts on change management, Harvard Business School professor John Kotter, acknowledges that many of the organisational change initiatives he has been involved in have failed. If the world's leading expert can't get it right, what hope is there for the rest of us?

Not surprisingly then, our attitude towards change is to ignore it. This, however, comes at a time when we can least afford to do so. Now, more than ever before, we need to be willing to be comfortable with change.

This is where VUCA comes into its own. VUCA can tell us just *how* the world is changing.

If we can move beyond our understanding of change as something that just happens (and something that we prefer to avoid), and instead learn to use VUCA's four parameters to identify *how* change happens, we can:

- understand change
- prepare for change
- leverage change to our advantage.

As Nathan Bennett and James Lemoine note in their 2014 *Harvard Business Review* article 'What VUCA Really Means for You', as long as we can go beyond using VUCA as a replacement term for *change*—that is, as a catch cry for 'Hey, it's crazy out there!', or as an excuse for doing nothing—in other words, 'What's the point, you can't prepare for a VUCA world anyway?'—the term can be incredibly useful for us.

How to understand change

In a 2014 article titled 'What's Going On' for the magazine *The American Interest*, editor Adam Garfinkle posed what he described as 'the uber question of our times': 'What the heck is going on, anyway?'

It's a fair enough question. People tend to ponder such issues during times of uncertainty. After posing his 'uber question', Garfinkle continues:

> It is now banal in the extreme to say that we are living in a rapidly changing world, and it can be misleading, too. The challenge is to understand how the world is changing, not how fast it is changing.

If the purpose of this book is to help improve the way in which you and your organisation adapt to change, then it's essential to also look at the conversations we have around the idea of change, and adapt them, too.

We previously identified the problem of change fatigue. But there is another, even bigger problem associated with change, and for this the management and leadership consultant industries have much to answer for.

A large degree of management and leadership thinking over the past half-century has revolved around the central idea of change as both a finite (with a beginning, middle and end) and a controllable or manageable process. Senior management implementing change? Great! A company-wide vision, perhaps, and a new org chart that nobody really understands. Now get on with your work, and never mention change, change management, or change implementation again ...

This, however, misses the point, which is this: as Greek philosopher Heraclitus once told us, the only thing constant in the world is change. So traditional change initiatives with fixed start and end points are not going to work and, besides, their existence in the first place suggests considerable hubris — to actually believe that change can be controlled and managed.

Rather than trying to manage change in the workplace, you and your organisation need to move with the change.

The right conversations about change aren't happening. Therefore, the right responses to change aren't happening either.

So — what to do? How do we manage ourselves within this landscape of constant change?

The three stages

Rather than just understanding VUCA as a concept, we can use it as a tool. How? We use the four VUCA parameters — volatility, uncertainty, complexity, ambiguity — with the three forces of the perfect storm — people, places, technology — in conjunction with a simple three-stage framework to understand exactly what we're up against.

The three-stage framework is to understand:

1. that change is happening
2. that change is happening faster
3. the exact nature of change.

Garfinkle's statement about banality and change is correct in observing the importance of understanding the nature of change. He is, however, a bit too quick to dismiss the need for each of us to accept that change actually is happening. Buy-in for stakeholders is not automatic; people process change in different ways and at different speeds, with some refusing to even accept it. Recognising this is an essential first step.

The first stage: Yes, it's actually happening

The first stage is understanding and then accepting that change is actually happening. While you may think for most people this is a given, for some it is not. In his beautifully irreverent book *The Game Changer*, motivation design expert Dr Jason Fox accurately diagnoses the problem:

'We love change, so long as it's not happening to us.'

Or this, from Intel Corporation's former chairman and CEO Andy Grove: 'With all the rhetoric about change, the fact is that we managers hate change, especially when it involves us.'

Be honest with yourself here: do you feel this way too?

The most obvious group of people who *didn't* love change was the Luddites, a group of nineteenth-century English textile workers. As they watched machines replace highly skilled artisans with unskilled (and therefore less expensive) labourers during the Industrial Revolution, the Luddites took to destroying the machinery in an attempt to stem the tide of change. The name 'Luddite' has now, of course, become synonymous with technological phobia and even ineptitude.

The Luddites' approach to change was not necessarily one of ignorance. It was more about personal interest and fear of how change would affect their wellbeing. But they failed to move beyond this first stage of understanding.

They failed to accept that change is a constant.

The second stage: Yes, it's getting quicker.

The second stage is understanding and accepting that the rate of change is increasing. There are two reasons why this is the case.

Firstly, our perception of change *changes* as we age. Remember when you were a kid at school, and the day would seemingly drag on forever? Now that you're older you find there is never enough time to fit all you need to do into the day.

It's normal for every human being to feel like the rate of change is getting faster: the older you become, the greater the increased sensation of change will be. Let's think about this in a bit more detail.

If you are 50 years old, you might be reading this book as a hard-copy paperback and underlining your favourite sentences with a pen and dog-earing important pages.

But if you are reading this book and you are 20 years old? Maybe the tablet is your normal. Paperbacks are the past—they're for strange people who sit in cafés; Luddites, if you will.

Thus, change is perceived at different rates by two age groups—yet it is happening at exactly the same pace in reality.

In a nutshell, the way we adapt to change is related to our perception of it. The better we understand this, the better our ability to adapt and succeed in a world that is essentially made of change.

But there is a second factor at play: irrespective of perception, change is happening faster.

This is primarily driven by technology, which is increasing the speed of all other forms of change.

While it's true that *some* technological advances have progressed in a relatively linear fashion—for example, the car (or the car until Tesla decided to take the wheel, pardon the pun), where the automobile industry has remained relatively static since the Model T Ford first rolled off Henry's production line over a hundred years ago—there are *many* other technologies that have increased exponentially.

The most well-known and often-cited example is computing power, where we use Moore's Law to describe the exponential growth evident in the past half-century. In the late 1960s Gordon Moore, a cofounder of Intel, the world's leading computer chip manufacturer, made the observation that the number of transistors that could be fitted onto a chip was doubling every two years or so, meaning that computer power was likewise doubling (this is known as *exponential growth*), and that computing costs were decreasing. This observation came to be known as Moore's Law, and to date it has proven incredibly accurate.

Given the ubiquity of technology today, we are looking at a world where change is increasingly rapid, and we have to both perceive and understand it in order to adapt to it.

The third stage: Yes, the world is becoming more volatile, uncertain, complex and ambiguous.

The third stage is understanding exactly *how* things are changing. This is what Garfinkle was getting at in the statement cited earlier.

As things change, we can use the lens of people, places and technology *and* the parameters of volatility, uncertainty, complexity and ambiguity to determine exactly *how* things are changing. With that understanding we can start to think about how we can adapt.

In the next chapter we'll go further into this third stage, looking into the eye of the storm to get a better understanding of how it's going to hit us.

Prediction and forecasting are becoming increasingly difficult and essentially a waste of time.

CHAPTER 2

The VUCA world

In this chapter we'll analyse the nature of change through:
- defining people, places and technology
- defining volatility, uncertainty, complexity and ambiguity
- examining how people, places and technology interact with VUCA factors
- understanding the Black Swan theory.

Every year during April and May, upwards of 30 commercial mountaineering teams gather at the Nepali and Tibetan base camps of Mount Everest. With most climbers spending between $30000 and $100000 to be guided up to the summit, it's a lucrative industry for a region that is otherwise very poor and has over 50 per cent of its population living on less than $2 a day.

During April the groups progressively install camps and fixed lines on the route in preparation for a relatively short but predictable window of calm weather that normally arrives in mid to late May. Outside of these months, virtually no-one climbs on Everest, because extremely strong winds (known as the jetstream) rake the mountain's upper slopes. When (or if) the weather window comes, all of the teams jockey for their shot at the top, resulting sometimes in excess of 100 climbers summiting in one day.

This strategy has been tried and tested over the past decade and a half and has proven to be relatively successful in getting people to the top—the success rate today is approximately 50 per cent (in other words, five in every ten who set out from Base Camp to reach the top do so).

Over this period, the number of climbers to have summited Everest has increased each season, from under 150 in 2000 to 658 climbers at the end of the 2013 season. Consistent with this is the death rate for climbers, down from 37 per cent from the period between 1922 to 1990 (as in for every 100 climbers who summited, 37 climbers died), to just under 4 per cent in the period since 1990.

Commercial expeditions operating on Mount Everest are much like most of our multinational corporations and organisations today: a great example of the benefits and efficacy of a reliance upon strategy, planning and fixed infrastructure when striving for success in stable and predictable environments.

But what happens when the environment becomes volatile and uncertain?

We see these commercial expeditions and organisations starting to break down. Strategy, planning and fixed infrastructure no longer work.

Don't believe me? Let's check out a few examples.

In 2005, the climbing season was marred by unseasonably unsettled weather, and the jetstream winds never really left the mountain. The normal weather window in late May simply never arrived. Although some teams did reach the summit, the total number of summits was down significantly on previous years. Those who went for the summit did so in questionable weather conditions and very late in the season. For some the gamble paid off, for others it did not: five climbers died that year (although not all of these deaths were attributable to the weather).

In 2008, the Chinese government closed access to the Tibetan side of the mountain for the whole season to enable them to carry the Olympic torch to the summit as part of the lead-in to the 2008 games (they broadcast it live to the world, but it was cloudy on the top). Other than the Chinese, no climbers summited from the Tibetan side that year.

In 2014, 16 Sherpas (including a very dear friend of mine, Ankaji Sherpa) were killed on Everest when a large serac (a house-sized piece of ice) collapsed and fell on them. This led to the closure of the mountain for the whole season from the Nepalese side, and very few summits for the year from the Tibetan side.

In 2015, a magnitude 7.8 earthquake struck Nepal, killing at least 7000 people. The earthquake caused an avalanche that hit Everest Base Camp, killing 19 climbers and support staff, and trapping hundreds more on the mountain for days. This led to another closed climbing season, with nobody summiting the mountain that year.

The strategy of commercial expeditions on Everest is to place as many paying climbers as possible on the summit (more climbers summiting means a better business reputation, and more clients in subsequent years, which means more profit).

In seasons of stable weather, this strategy is successful. However, when things become volatile and uncertain—when unexpected events such as unseasonal weather and avalanches and earthquakes occur—the strategy falls apart. The true nature of the strategy is revealed: too linear, too rigid and unable to tolerate the unexpected. (Of course, the fact that any of the events mentioned earlier are considered by many climbers in the Himalaya, the highest mountain range on earth, as being 'unexpected' goes to show just how blinded and obsessed people can become by their own linear thinking and strategy.)

So we're beginning to see that the traditional way of doings might not be well suited for the new landscape of uncertainty and volatility.

However, before we delve into understanding more about the problems and risks associated with traditional linear structures (be they commercial mountaineering expeditions or multinational commercial organisations), it's important that we get a good understanding of exactly what the causes of VUCA are.

The three forces

In the first chapter we learned that the approaching perfect storm is comprised of three forces: people, places and technology. Let's have a deeper look at each of these forces.

People

With a global population now in excess of 7 billion, it's no wonder that people are a major contributor to the perfect storm. Despite such a wide array of religions and cultures, it is still surprising just how determined we seem to be to disagree with one another. At a time when we have access to more information than ever before, and have an unprecedented ability to connect and communicate with each other on a global scale, we are ironically at risk of becoming even more closed-minded and reluctant to embrace the magnificent diversity amongst us.

This of course makes perfect sense when you consider inequality. Global charity Oxfam suggests that 1 per cent of the world's population owns 50 per cent of the world's wealth, and that the 80 richest people on earth have the same wealth as the poorest 50 per cent of the global population.

However, with almost 3.5 billion people now having access to the internet (up from just 360 million in 2000), and with this number estimated to double by the year 2020 (with most of the growth coming from developing countries), everything is going to change, on a global scale. Figuratively speaking, a much flatter and more transparent world will appear, and everything, from the way we socialise to the way we do our work, will be different.

Places

As the majority of world's population comes online over the next five years, the reach of globalisation will be broader than ever before. Geographically isolated countries such as Australia, where we have had a tendency to see ourselves as being somewhat removed from the rest of the world, will find that the rest of the world has arrived on our doorstep. The world will be more accessible than ever before.

And not only is the world changing metaphorically, it's also changing physically. In 2014 and 2015, the world experienced its two hottest years ever recorded. There is unequivocal evidence that a change in our climate is underway, and this is going to have massive ramifications around the world. How we use energy, how we access water and where we grow our food will become global issues, not just national ones.

And despite this, we still fool ourselves into thinking we can control the world around us. In 2015, the Indonesian resort island of Bali saw what has become a somewhat familiar phenomenon: a volcanic ash cloud causing major disruption to international air travel. No flights could get in or out of Denpasar's airport, and thousands of tourists—predominantly Australians—were 'stranded' in their resorts. Social media was flooded with the hashtag #stuckinBali. The stranded tourists expended more energy complaining to airlines, travel agencies and various insurance companies than they spent on their actual holidays. And the end result? Very little.

Nothing can fight nature, not even the internet.

People, combined with places, can make for stormy weather, and sometimes not even technology can assist.

Technology

Of course, while a combination of people and places is a potent mix, the force that is really amplifying the magnitude of the perfect storm is technology. Its current rate of growth is dizzyingly spectacular — and as we will learn in this book, it won't be slowing down anytime soon — rather, it's only going to get faster.

Technology is the key driving force behind the perfect storm. In 2020, it is estimated that more than half of the world's population will be using internet-enabled mobile devices. That'll be nearly 4 billion people with smartphones, and each of these smartphones will have in them more computing power than all of NASA had when it first put Neil Armstrong and Buzz Aldrin on the moon in 1969. Think about that for a minute. That's the equivalent of 4 billion NASAs in the pockets and hands of half of the world's population. Yes, things are about to get crazy.

Again, imagine the profound impact this is going to have on everything we do, from the way we socialise to the way we work to the way we communicate our stories to the world. For example, with an estimated 100 million Chinese citizens now using Sina Weibo (a social media/microblogging platform), imagine the outcome of the events of Tiananmen Square had they happened in 2015, rather than 1989. Would history have changed course? Or would it simply have been 100 million times worse, because technology, combined with people and places — the three forces of the perfect storm creating the VUCA world — made it so?

Breaking down VUCA

One of the problems with any new word that enters the business lexicon is that can be prone to misuse—and VUCA is no exception. A quick review of current literature on the VUCA topic reveals this to be the case—the best example being 'VUCA Prime'. Flipping the VUCA acronym on its head, with volatility yielding to vision, uncertainty yielding to understanding, complexity yielding to clarity and ambiguity yielding to agility, this convenient retrofitting by those in the management consulting and leadership industry fails to offer any meaningful solution.

VUCA is at risk of becoming a 'cool' way of talking about change, and will no doubt soon sit alongside current title-holders *disruption*, *innovation* and *agility*, all of which are very much in vogue right now (particularly among big corporations that include these words in their vision statements—but can any of them actually articulate what these words mean and look like in everyday practice?).

So rather than using VUCA as a superficial descriptor of the changing world, it's important to really understand the characteristics of each of the four components of VUCA. So that's what we're going to do now.

Volatility

Something likely to change in a sudden or extreme way is described as being volatile. The word is derived from the Latin *volatilis*, which means *to fly away* (in chemistry, volatility is the rate at which a chemical changes from a solid to a vapour state; volatility increases with temperature and decreases with pressure). In broader terms and as it relates to VUCA, volatility is used to describe the rapid price fluctuations of securities (note that the share market volatility index is commonly referred to as the 'fear index'), currencies and commodities and, more recently, deteriorating social and geopolitical situations.

What does volatility look like out there in the real word? Here are five recent examples:

1. Australia has had *five* prime ministers in the past five years. In the 32-year period prior to that, we had only four.
2. The S&P 500 annualised volatility index (widely known as the VIX) has averaged 21 per cent since 2008. During the period from 1983 to 2007, the VIX averaged only 15 per cent, *despite* the 1987 and 2001 dotcom crashes.
3. There has been a dramatic increase in extreme weather events and hotter, dryer periods (2014 and 2015 were the hottest years ever recorded).
4. The events of the Arab Spring led to the demise of four rulers, a civil war in Syria, the rise of the Islamic State, and a massive refugee crisis in Europe.
5. Facebook in 2014 acquired instant messaging app WhatsApp (a start-up tech company that didn't even exist in 2008, with only 55 employees) for $19 billion.

Uncertainty

Something that is unreliable, not known, or not definite is described as being uncertain. The word is derived from the Latin *certus*, which means *to sift, discern and decide*; the negative of this being an inability to sift, discern or decide. Uncertainty leads to difficulty in forecasting and making predictions, and often results in so-called experts making dramatically different predictions from one another despite working off the same information.

What does uncertainty look like out there in the real word? Here are five recent examples, and the questions they pose:

1. The ebola outbreak in West Africa in 2014 and 2015: would it spread to other continents and create a global pandemic?
2. The ongoing Eurozone crisis: would Greece default on its debt, leading to another global banking crisis?
3. The civil war in Ukraine: has Russia's support of the Ukrainian separatists proven that we have entered another period of global destabilisation?
4. The US became the world's largest producer of hydrocarbons in 2013 (only five years earlier the US was a net importer of hydrocarbons): is the dominance of OPEC finished?
5. The rise of China and its large military forces: what does this mean for geopolitical stability in the Pacific region?

Complexity

Something that has many integrated, interdependent parts and is difficult to understand is described as complex. The word is derived from the Latin *complexus*, which means *totality*. Complexity occurs where many interdependent parts comprise one or multiple systems: a *totality* of parts. As technology-driven interconnections between markets, economies and populations continues to increase, so too will levels of complexity.

The ease of accessibility to, and prevalence of, big data has only increased this level of complexity, and will continue to do so at an ever-quickening pace.

What does complexity look like out there in the real word? Here are five recent examples:

1. The US subprime mortgage crisis, which led to the GFC, the Eurozone crisis and numerous other global economic woes.
2. The 2011 earthquake in Japan that created the tsunami that led to the Fukushima incident, leading to a shutdown of all of Japanese nuclear power plants for four years, Germany abandoning its nuclear power program, and the uranium price collapsing by more than 50 per cent.
3. The United Nations' attempts to manage global carbon emissions and consider the demands of both developed and developing nations.
4. Governments trying to meet their own requirements to regulate an ever-increasing number of 'sharing economy' businesses such as Uber and Airbnb.
5. The evolution of China as a global superpower and ongoing tensions surrounding claims to islands in the South China Sea.

Ambiguity

Something that has multiple meanings or lacks clarity is described as being ambiguous. The word is derived from the Latin *ambigere*, which means *to be undecided*. While the concept of uncertainty relates to things that are unknown, ambiguity describes things that have potentially multiple known outcomes (but it's unclear *which* of the outcomes will occur).

What does ambiguity look like out there in the real word? Here are five recent examples, and the questions they pose:

1. Have we ensured a sustainable recovery from the GFC or has the 'can' just been kicked further down the road?
2. Will the world's economies ever come to grips with the need to massively reduce carbon emissions to prevent catastrophic global warming, or is it already too late?
3. Will cryptocurrencies such as the Bitcoin become the new currency of choice?
4. Just exactly which jobs that we take for granted today will be performed by automation or artificial intelligence in ten years time?
5. How concerned should we be about military artificial intelligence? (In July 2015 more than 1000 artificial intelligence experts and researchers, including Elon Musk, Steve Wozniak and Stephen Hawking, warned of a forthcoming military artificial intelligence arms race.)

Black Swans

It would be remiss at this point to not discuss the work of author, trader and anti-academic Nassim Nicholas Taleb, who writes about Black Swan events, which he describes as highly consequential but unlikely occurrences that render predictions and standard explanations meaningless. In other words, Taleb writes about the perfect storm called VUCA.

The Black Swan concept has its roots in Latin and the Roman poet Juvenal, who wrote of rare events as being like 'a rare bird in the lands and very much like a black swan'. This phrase took hold in Europe in the 1600s, when it was used as a statement of impossibility. It wasn't until 1697 when Dutch explorer Willem de Vlamingh landed in Western Australia (where I grew up—we once had a black swan land in my parents' front garden, and I can confirm that they have a nasty bite) and noted the presence of black swans that the phrase gained an even deeper irony.

Just because you've never seen a black swan before doesn't mean it doesn't exist.

Taleb suggests that most major world events are of the Black Swan variety, including the First and Second World Wars, the advent of the personal computer and the internet, 9/11 and the 2008 GFC. The success of Apple and Facebook are another two examples.

Taleb argues that despite our natural bias, it is a mistake to predict the likelihood of future events based on the past; in other words, the past is not always a reliable indicator of the future. He then points out that many of our societal systems (and our organisations, I might add) are designed to meet worst-case scenarios based on past events.

The Fukushima nuclear accident in Japan is a case in point. The height of the protective seawalls around the plant was based on a wave height from the largest previously recorded tsunami (which measured just under 10 metres), but the tsunami that hit in 2011 was 13 metres high, making it the largest one ever recorded in Japan.

Building something based on past history does not necessarily mean that it will be suited to future events, and that goes for our organisations, too.

These Black Swan events are essentially statistical outliers, and therein lies the problem: we ignore them for exactly that reason. But it is from these outliers that we can learn the most, and with increased volatility, uncertainty, complexity and ambiguity occurring between people, places and technology, outliers are not going to be so unusual anymore. Remember again the earlier statement: *just because you've never seen a black swan before doesn't mean it doesn't exist.*

The avalanche at Everest Base Camp in 2015 was a classic case of the Black Swan. As we read at the beginning of this chapter, every year somewhere between 500 and 800 climbers and support staff set up camp for between eight and ten weeks at the foot of the mountain. Countless thousands of trekkers also visit the site every year. People have been doing it since 1952 when the Swiss first opened up the route. And, prior to 2015, was the location of Base Camp thought to be safe from the daily avalanches that come off the surrounding peaks of Everest, Nuptse, Pumori and Lingtren? Absolutely.

But now? Perhaps not so much.

Nobody ever thought that such a large avalanche would occur, because it never had previously.

It's like the perfect storm. No-one ever thought it could happen, because it's never happened before either.

It's probably the right time to check in and ask you an important question: Is all of this starting to make you feel just a bit … uncomfortable?

If it is, it's okay—that's a normal response. You did, after all, grow up in the old world. In the next chapter, we'll investigate that response further.

It shows just how difficult we find it to let go of the old comfortable ways of doing things and embrace the volatility of the new world order.

CHAPTER 3

The old world

In this chapter, we'll look at how our psychology interacts with a VUCA world through:
- seeing why we prefer the status quo
- examining the Comfort Paradox
- showing what happens to our psyches when confronted with a VUCA world
- predicting what might happen if we fail to adapt—or if we succeed.

In 2008 cable television network HBO ran a series that has achieved a cult status among fans of quality television miniseries. Called *Generation Kill*, it was the (very lightly) fictionalised story of the US Marine Corps' First Reconnaissance Division and its role in the second Iraqi invasion of 2003 (or, as it was known, 'Operation Iraqi Freedom').

Generation Kill was based on the book and series of articles by *Rolling Stone* journalist Evan Wright, who embedded with First Recon for their entire campaign, from first footfall in mid March to entry into Baghdad in early April.

Reconnaissance marines are among the elite warriors of the US military. They are trained, much like alpine-style mountaineers, to move light and fast and to adapt quickly to their changing surroundings. What they don't do is move in large numbers, and definitely not in slow, methodical, predictable formations.

That changed with Operation Iraqi Freedom. First Recon was sent in-country in lightly armoured open-top Humvees, with no air cover, in broad daylight, across swathes of open desert, en masse. It was not First Recon's preferred way of doing things.

For an organisation such as the US military (which had so clearly identified the VUCA threat in the first place) to work in such a manner shows just how difficult we find it to let go of the old comfortable ways of doing things and embrace the volatility of the new world order.

But what exactly is comfort?

The opposite of VUCA

For most of us, comfort in life comes from:

- stability
- certainty
- simplicity
- clarity.

Does this sound boring? Then you are very much out of the ordinary. Think about it a little more.

Politicians often talk about *stability* when seeking election to government; we vote an unstable or volatile government out of office. The daily weather forecast reassures us about certainty in weather patterns; it allows us to plan and prepare. There are no nasty surprises. Why do scientific and business reports start with abstracts or executive summaries? Because we like complex ideas to be streamlined, broken down, simplified. Why do you use a map? Because we always like *clarity* in relation to where we are. (Who enjoys being lost?)

If we gave stability, certainty, simplicity and clarity an acronym, it would be SCSC, but it's not very catchy; besides, we don't need a new name for it, because it already has one: it's called the status quo, and the human race is fiercely protective of it.

Be that as it may, the status quo is on the way out. For good. As you can see in figure 3.1, it's in direct opposition to the VUCA world.

Figure 3.1: status quo vs. VUCA

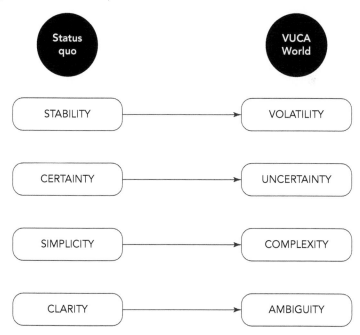

The Comfort Paradox

There is an economic theory known as the Jevons Paradox that can be applied to the old world order versus new ways of doing things in business.

The Jevons Paradox is named for William Stanley Jevons, who in 1865 asserted that energy-efficient steam engines had caused an efficiency dilemma by inadvertently accelerating Britain's consumption of coal.

In other words, the newly invented steam engine (a form of technological progress) had increased the efficiency with which a resource—coal—was being used, but an unanticipated consequence of this was that the *rate of consumption* of that resource had risen because of an increasing demand for train services.

It's a double-edged sword, and we can also call it by another name: the Comfort Paradox.

The Comfort Paradox is a problem, and it's a problem entirely of our own making. Figure 3.2 illustrates it.

Figure 3.2: the Comfort Paradox

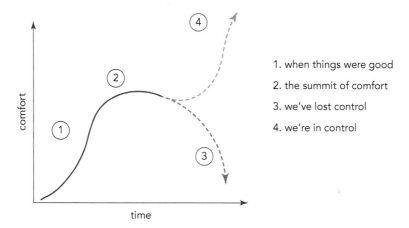

1. when things were good
2. the summit of comfort
3. we've lost control
4. we're in control

Why? Because it's in our DNA to improve our lot in life, and to increase our level of comfort.

Think of Maslow's Hierarchy of Needs. Maslow's model states there are five progressive stages that a human is motivated to reach. The most basic stage is having our biological and physiological needs met: food, water, shelter and sleep, through to security and safety—until we reach the top of the hierarchy and self-actualisation.

Humanity's relentless drive towards technical innovation and sophistication is all about enabling the ease with which we secure each of our five needs.

We use technology as our primary means to move through the stages. The irony is that in our efforts to make ourselves more comfortable and stable—to reach the top of the hierarchy—we are actually making ourselves *less* comfortable.

That's the Comfort Paradox.

If you don't agree, that's understandable. There are, after all, many examples of how our standards of living have improved significantly due to technological advancement. For example, current predictions have cancer eradicated by the year 2025. Some are even suggesting the Baby Boomer generation will be the last generation of people to die, *period*, such are the predicted radical improvements in health care and preservation of life.

Notwithstanding all of this, technological innovation also brings undeniable negatives.

Every day we see examples of where the use of technology designed to improve our standard of living paradoxically *undermines* our comfort and our ability to meet Maslow's five needs:

- the constant improvement in smartphone technology creates status anxiety about owning the latest smartphone model
- the inescapable connectivity of social media creates an epidemic of Facebook childhood bullying and gives terrorist groups such as Islamic State a forum to disseminate horrific, cinema-quality videos
- all of our modern comforts come at the price of global warming, which is increasingly evident.

Most of this comes from technology unavailable just a decade ago.

Long-term change for good brings short-term pain.

The problems with exponentiality

As the interplay between people, places and technology continues, and the growth rate in the development of technology, particularly computing power, continues to grow exponentially, it is in the space between linearity and exponentiality that our human discomfort occurs, as shown in figure 3.3.

Figure 3.3: exponential discomfort

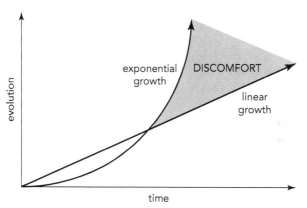

Part of the problem with the VUCA world is that exponential growth is a concept humans find very hard to understand.

Someone who *does* understand the concept pretty well is inventor, futurist, author and director of engineering at Google, Ray Kurzweil (whom *Forbes* magazine describes as 'the ultimate thinking machine'—that's a pretty cool moniker). Kurzweil uses an analogy of firstly taking 30 linear steps (where the distance of each step is the same as the last), and then taking 30 exponential steps (where the distance of each step is double that of the previous).

The distance travelled by taking 30 linear steps is approximately 20 to 30 metres (depending on the length of your legs). This might get you from one end of your house to the other, or across a busy city street. However, taking 30 exponential steps gets you around the world *25 times* (a distance of about a million kilometres) or to the moon and back again. Hard to believe, right?

As the growth of technology increases exponentially, it will do so at a rate we cannot imagine.

And therein lies the problem. We just can't comprehend it. Our inability to keep up with the current rate of change, let alone be able to *imagine* what the future might look like, causes us to feel anxious and overwhelmed. It's like sitting down and trying to contemplate the dimensions of the universe: the brain becomes quickly overloaded.

The three symptoms of VUCA

As we have identified, rapid change, the type that is the norm in the VUCA world, isn't something we can easily comprehend. When faced with its impact, it's not surprising that we don't understand it. We react with:

- dissonance
- entropy
- disengagement.

Think of something that has happened to you that was so unexpected, so utterly incomprehensible, that even now you look back and think, 'How could that have happened?'

For some people this might be the terrorist attack on the World Trade Center in New York and on the Pentagon in Washington, DC on 9/11. Even now, many years on from that infamous day, it is hard for most people who witnessed the events, whether first hand or as they were broadcast live around the world, to forget their feelings. Feelings that were for the most part disbelief and horror. *How* could such a thing be happening?

Dissonance

The cause of this disbelief is known in psychology as *cognitive dissonance*. Cognitive dissonance occurs when the brain struggles to interpret new information that does not correlate with or confirm the existing knowledge or beliefs that the brain already possesses.

On that day in New York in 2001, and indeed all around the world, cognitive dissonance was occurring en masse.

In a more subtle kind of way, due to the interconnectedness of people, places and technology, cognitive dissonance is once again happening en masse. In fact, it is *de rigueur* for the VUCA world. As everything changes at an ever-increasing speed, the frequency of occasions where the brain receives information that does not correlate with existing knowledge will increase continually.

Cognitive dissonance is the root cause of people's discomfort in the VUCA world.

Entropy

Operating in tandem with cognitive dissonance is the concept of *psychic entropy*, first introduced by psychologist Mihály Csíkszentmihályi (surname pronounced 'six-cent-mi-hal-yi').

According to Csíkszentmihályi, entropy occurs whenever information from the surrounding environment disrupts our consciousness by threatening its goals. This in turn leads to a disorganisation of the self, impaired effectiveness and, ultimately, an internal self so weakened it cannot invest attention or pursue its goals.

This idea is based on the premise that every piece of information our brains receive is evaluated for its impact on our psyche: the information is run through a filter to determine whether it supports or threatens our goals, and whether or not it is congruent with our beliefs. A self (or psyche) that becomes so weakened that it cannot invest attention or pursue its goals is not going to do well in a VUCA world.

Let's go back to 9/11. Like many others, in the days that followed, I didn't feel like doing much at all. I was due to travel to New Zealand a few months later to undertake a mountaineering training course but at the time I remember thinking 'What's the point?' And I know I wasn't the only one thinking that. For example, the Association of Surfing Professionals cancelled all but one of the remaining men's world title events for the year after the attacks.

Entropy only serves to intensify and compound the seeming disorder of VUCA. The compounding of the external VUCA world with the internal dissonance of the human mind ultimately creates an internal malaise.

In the old world order, when the status quo reigned, our minds were able to make sense of the outside world, and it was for the most part consistent with our expectations. In other words, cognitive dissonance and entropy were relatively infrequent occurrences. When they did occur, they occurred so infrequently and with such limited magnitude that they could be handled.

In the VUCA world, it is common to experience entropy, because much of the information we receive threatens our goals and reduces our opportunity for comfort. And when our opportunities for comfort are under threat, we become incredibly anxious and uneasy. We are less likely to retain self control in this state and are more likely to react to our circumstances. Simply put, VUCA is not the ideal operating environment for people.

Disengagement

In the immediate hours after 9/11, and after grasping the enormity of the situation, many retreated from the horror of the world. They disengaged.

In times of unexpected events, when cognitive dissonance and entropy run rife, we have a tendency to withdraw from the world at large and revert to our closest and most important social groups, normally our immediate family and friends.

The Kübler-Ross model is a framework that proposes five emotional stages through which a person passes when grieving. The stages are *denial*, *anger*, *bargaining*, *depression* and *acceptance*. In those hours and days after 9/11, I suspect most were either in denial or anger.

Could it be that we now are grieving our loss of the old world, the loss of our comfort? If so, at which point of the grief cycle do we currently sit?

Cognitive dissonance and entropy are not the only causes of disengagement. There is another cause and symptom of the VUCA world—that of information overload—that also leads to disengagement.

There is currently much talk about the need to invest in big data. Big data is a broad term for data sets so large or complex that traditional data processing applications are inadequate. In 2014 IBM estimated that every day we create 2.5 *billion* gigabytes of data, meaning that more than 90 per cent of data in existence today was created in the last two years alone.

As an example, Google's self-driving car gathers 750 megabytes (nearly one gigabyte) of sensory data per second. That means that in your average daily commute of 30 minutes to work, the Google car will be capturing 1350 gigabytes of data!

If we apply this to the world of business, the information overload is so overwhelming that we cannot process what is going on with our usual status quo approach, because it is simply not adequate. So—we switch off. We just don't bother to understand the data anymore.

And this is a problem. Because in the VUCA world, that big data is coming in thick and fast. And it's getting more complex at an exponential rate.

A crafted future?

So we now know how a VUCA world affects our mindset. If our mindset doesn't change, what kind of a future are we looking at?

In her book *The Shift: The Future of Work is Already Here*, London Business School Professor Lynda Gratton presents two variants of the future of work. Similar to the movie *Sliding Doors*, Gratton has two scenarios: the Default Future and the Crafted Future.

For the Default Future Gratton tells the story of Jill, living in London and working for a large global organisation. Overwhelm, discomfort and reactivity is her norm. Her frantic and fragmented life in 2025 shows that a combination of people, places and technology has created a constantly 'on', 24/7 world, leaving her repeatedly bombarded by requests for her time, with little space to concentrate, observe, think and play. Gratton also tells the story of Briana, a member of the working poor in the American Midwest, whose life is shaped by repeated economic bubbles and crashes, and the ongoing replacement of non- and semi-skilled work by technology and the better educated workforces of India and China.

The Default Future is one of isolation, fragmentation, exclusion and narcissism, where no-one works together.

People are chronically overwhelmed; world events and technological change outpace the required actions and remedies. Essentially, this default scenario is a future where people have not been able to adapt or cope, and can't possibly excel.

In other words, they haven't been able to adapt to the VUCA world. They have attempted to manage it by fighting the elements of the perfect storm—people, places, and technology—but they are fighting a losing battle.

In mountaineering terms, they have been blown off the mountain.

It is the Comfort Paradox writ large.

In the second scenario, which she refers to as the Crafted Future, Gratton tells of Miguel, who lives in Rio de Janeiro. His working day in 2025 is a stimulating mix of real space and virtual engagement with a geographically distributed but interdependent team of planning specialists working on a submission to help reduce traffic congestion in a northern city in India. His work is interesting and meaningful. We also hear the story of Xui Li, who lives in Zhengzhou, China. Xui Li is an independent micro-entrepreneur who sells her hand-crafted dresses across the world via an online sales and distribution cooperative with a vast international reach.

Collaboration plays a key role in the Crafted Future, where choice and wisdom contribute to a balanced way of working. This future comprises of good decisions, rapid adoption of good ideas and people taking advantage of technologies and working together in light and fast teams; it is an environment where work can truly be of value and appreciated.

This is the future where all have adapted to the VUCA world and embraced the opportunities presented by the combination of people, places and technology, rather than becoming anxious and overwhelmed by the discomfort it brings.

Xui Li and Miguel have been climbing the mountain alpine style, light and fast. They have embraced the perfect storm and are using it to their advantage.

Idyllic predictions of a futuristic tech-enabled utopia are often criticised for being far-fetched and naive, and to an extent, this is understandable. But as the saying goes, with great power comes great responsibility, and the same thing applies to technology. What Gratton is saying is this: we *do* have a choice as to how we use it.

It's a choice between sitting back, throwing our hands up in the air and giving up, or proactively taking action and making sure that the Default Future is not our own.

We have the option to craft our future.

So the challenge ahead of us is this: how we can achieve a Crafted Future in our lives and our organisations? First we need to gain a better understanding of our organisations, and appreciate that they are the primary structures upon which our society depends—why are they the way they are, and will they help us achieve a Crafted Future? The next chapter will do just that.

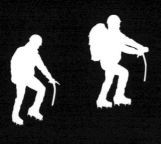

The majority of organisations today are operating with a static and outdated design and structure.

CHAPTER 4

How we got so organised

In this chapter we'll get into a central part of most people's working world—the organisation—and discuss:
- the linear organisation's incompatibility with the VUCA landscape
- the history of the organisation
- the strategy- and goal-focussed approach of today's organisations
- the approach traditional organisations are taking to cope with the VUCA landscape
- the management and leadership consultant industry as an inadequate response to these conditions.

In the mid 1980s, the nascent mobile phone industry had a problem: phone coverage was too expensive to provide outside of urban areas. As a solution, an international consortium headed by Motorola developed an offshoot called Iridium, with a plan to launch 77 low-earth-orbit satellites to provide satellite phone coverage to any location on Earth.

While Iridium deployed some very clever technology, the project cost a lot of money: nearly $6 billion. Handsets weren't cheap either, coming at about at $3000 each, with call costs between $6 and $30 a minute.

Iridium had designed their system in the mid 1980s, but with an incredibly long lead time they failed to appreciate that:

- the cost of installing mobile phone towers was decreasing
- network speeds were increasing exponentially.

By the time the phone service was launched in 1998 (with American Vice President Al Gore making the first call), more than a decade after the idea was first conceived, Iridium was in dire financial straits.

With a poor user experience, outsized fees and reports of organisational mismanagement, Iridium filed for Chapter 11 bankruptcy only one year after the service began. *Air and Space Magazine* went as far as to describe Iridium as 'the greatest dog ever launched into space'.

It was an obscenely costly mistake and is an excellent example of long-term business strategy ignoring the evidence when it is incongruent with its objectives. In other words, an excellent example of how slow, methodical, single-minded pursuit of an unchanging goal doesn't work in the VUCA world.

Interestingly, and despite a net asset valuation of $6 billion, the company was subsequently purchased by a very savvy group of investors for $25 million. After a significant restructuring the new business was publicly listed on the Nasdaq and has since been highly profitable, thanks to its utility to the US military and smaller entities (including alpinists) conducting work in the remote parts of the globe.

As confronting as it might sound, many of today's large commercial organisations are just as exposed as Iridium was to the perfect storm of VUCA. For our organisations to survive, we need to understand why.

VUCA and the linear organisation

As Ray Kurzweil says, 'An invention needs to make sense in the world in which it is finished, not the world in which it is started'. It's an apt summation of the problem facing many large organisations today.

Organisations are cumbersome in nature, a consequence of their hierarchical, linear structure. Many do not allow for the rapid deployment of products and services. In addition, a preference for quantitative metrics over qualitative results has led to some organisations forgetting their most important resource: people (both the employee and the customer).

David S. Rose is an American technology entrepreneur and the CEO of Gust, a platform connecting early-stage start-ups with angel investors. In his book *Angel Investing,* he makes the following alarming statement: 'Any company designed for success in the twentieth century is doomed to failure in the twenty-first.'

If you disagree with this sentiment, then I think you have your head buried deeply in the sand.

As we progress further into the twenty-first century, the evidence in support of this statement is both compelling and ever increasing.

The list of once-great organisations that are either gone or shells of their former selves grows longer by the day: Kodak. Motorola. Nokia. BlackBerry. Dell. Yahoo. Sony. MySpace. Blockbuster. McDonalds. HMV. Borders. Angus & Robertson.

All of these organisations were highly linear in nature. They ignored the warning signs of the VUCA world. They all chose a traditional approach when it came to their thinking about the future. They all neglected to understand, perceive, or adapt to change.

Serious cause for alarm

Babson College, one of the USA's leading private business schools, in 2011 predicted that, by 2021, 40 per cent of existing Fortune 500 companies would no longer exist.

Others have made similar alarming predictions. In 2011, global strategy and innovation company Innosight noted the average lifespan of an S&P 500 company had decreased from 67 years in the 1920s to 15 years today. They predicted that at the current churn rate, 75 per cent of companies on the S&P 500 would be replaced by 2027.

It's not just big American companies either. On a 2014 business trip to Silicon Valley, David Thodey, former CEO of Australian communications giant Telstra (with a market cap of $7 billion) spoke of industry insiders telling him bluntly that his business model was 'dead'.

In a newspaper interview in 2015, Thodey noted he didn't worry about the recent developments within the Australian telecoms sector (Telstra's main competition is now TPG, an acquisitions-hungry business with a market cap of approximately $8 billion); rather he spent more time talking about smaller third-tier competition and new innovative start-ups.

Designed for yesterday

The root of the problem for today's traditional organisations is this: they were designed to operate in the old world order, where status quo was the norm. Structured in a hierarchical fashion and fit for a linear world, the organisations were designed to be robust and resilient to change, but not *adaptable* to change. Designed to strictly control people from the top down, to acquire and rely on physical assets and to profit from scarcity. The bottom line was king, irrespective of how it was reached.

But as we now know, not only is technology within the new world order changing exponentially, but so too is everything else: the way that people live and work. So our organisations are in desperate need of an understanding of that change, and an ability to keep abreast with the pace and shock of the new.

Before we identify what this change might look like, however, it's important we understand just a little about the history of organisations; they have, after all, become an integral part of the status quo.

The Visible Hand

During the 1850s, transportation in North America was revolutionised by a massive railway-building boom. Dramatically reducing travel times and costs across the continent, the boom opened up the territories of Dakota, Montana and beyond to those looking for gold and grazing land. Railroads replaced the horse and cart as the primary means of personal transport and the distribution of goods. Travel times from New York to New Orleans, for example, were reduced from approximately five weeks in 1800 to two weeks in 1830—and just five days by 1857. For the distribution of goods, railroads proved to be three to five times more efficient than canals, which were previously the primary method of distribution.

Alfred Chandler describes this transformation in his Pulitzer Prize–winning 1977 book *The Visible Hand: The Managerial Revolution in American Business*. Chandler describes the large-scale coordination required to integrate many different regional railroads into a single national transportation system: no prior business or enterprise had ever required such control and coordination over such a diverse array of tasks and scheduling. This required such levels of coordination and standardising of procedures and technology that *administrative* forces were proved to be of greater strength and cost efficiency than *market* forces, thus making the organisation the primary means for productivity and economic growth.

Chandler refers to the salaried executives and middle management who emerged within these organisations as the 'visible hand', which subsequently became the guiding force in global economics, and has continued to be so until this day.

The *multiunit enterprise*, which is how Chandler refers to these new organisations, and *multidivisional enterprises* (multiunit enterprises—developed in the 1920s—nested underneath 'parent' companies that are themselves multiunit enterprises), became the two key organisational types on which the majority of organisational management thinking and consulting has been based. This means today's traditional organisations are still using designs—and methods, in some cases—that are either 100 or 150 years old.

The key point here isn't that this organisational design is old; after all, we take wisdom from the philosophy of the Greeks and Romans (think of Heraclitus and his concept of the constancy of change). Rather, it's the fact that, *despite* the designs being either 100 or 150 years old, they have *hardly changed at all*. There has been very little evolution.

The majority of organisations today, those that ensure society continues to function on a daily basis, are operating with a static and outdated design and structure.

It's no wonder we fear change!

The birth of the management consultant

Alongside the evolution of the organisation, and perhaps as an early indication that organisations were not inherently natural and efficient structures, there sprang an industry of consultants looking to 'improve' the way in which organisations did their work.

They are formally called management consultants. (They do, informally, have several other monikers.)

The industry tackled 'improvements', firstly from a strategy perspective, and more recently from a leadership perspective. This service industry has its origins in 1910 with Frederick Taylor's 'scientific management' method, which ultimately led to the development of large international consultancy businesses, the two most recognised of course being McKinsey and Company and Boston Consulting Group (BCG).

In conjunction with the development of these large consultancies, management academics and thinkers such as Peter Drucker, Michael Porter and John Kotter were developing new concepts of strategy to improve organisational performance. Strategy models currently still in favour include McKinsey and Company's 7S Framework (36 years old), Porter's Five Forces Analysis (also 36 years old) and Kotter's Eight Steps to Change (celebrating its twentieth birthday).

Strategic, yes. Outdated? Just a bit.

The linear strategy

In his insightful book *Corpus Rios: The How and What of Business Strategy*, consultant Christopher Tipler describes the current state of strategic planning: if God laughs at plans, 'God must find business hilarious, because businesses make a lot of plans'.

Tipler's book is very much a critique of the current state of strategic planning in organisations, identifying a number of woes, including unnecessary complicatedness and unreliability, dysfunctional use of 'stultifying language' and protection of the status quo through silos and budgets, aversion to risk (and hence opportunity), and lack of imagination.

The traditional approach to strategy and planning has consisted of the following minimum ingredients. It:

- is undertaken by the organisation's senior management or executive team
- has identified specific objectives
- has identified timelines (e.g. a five-year plan, with a beginning and an end point)

- has numbered, incremental, prescriptive steps identified and committed to.

The propensity for linear strategy has to a large extent guided most other things within today's organisations.

If the key guiding premise of an organisation is its strategy, and if that strategy is ordered, prescriptive, quantified and linear, it follows that everything else the organisation does will have the same linear characteristics.

According to Dan Colussy, who masterminded the rescue and buyout of Iridium in 2000, the business plan was the main reason for Iridium's disaster:

> The Iridium business plan was locked in place twelve years before the system became operational … the idea was that a businessman would carry this thing around the world in his briefcase and dial home … Of course by the time it got up, nobody needed it …

In his book *Light Footprint Management*, consultant Charles-Édouard Bouée says, 'Businesses need to adapt by dispensing with old ideas, such as the assumption that the task of management is to seek adaptation to equilibrium. There is no equilibrium'.

An unhealthy obsession with goals

To achieve an organisation's strategic objective, a series of plans will be implemented. As you can see in figure 4.1 (overleaf), and are probably familiar with in your own organisation, this is a very linear process.

Figure 4.1: typical strategic plan

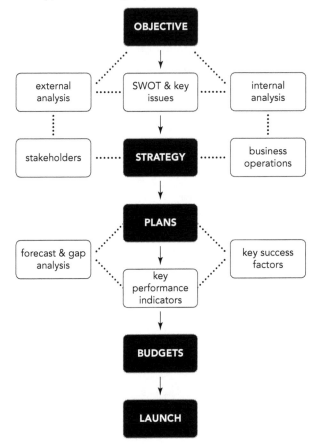

As we learn in chapter 6, however, such reliance upon prescriptive and linear strategies and plans is less than ideal: teams are particularly prone to 'goalodicy', where goals and objectives become such an obsession that they lead to poor decisions and outcomes (and ironically, the goals and objectives not being achieved).

Goalodicy can lead a team to become so attached to their goals that they start to define the team's identity. This in turn causes the group to become blinded to real world feedback and ignore the warning signs that continued pursuit of the goal may no longer the best option.

In his very clever book *The Antidote*, journalist Oliver Burkeman describes a study of New York taxi drivers who were so focussed on their goals they were effectively blinded by them. In NYC, it was a widely held belief that cabs are more difficult to catch on rainy days than when the weather is fine. The cause of this was commonly attributed to all the cabs being busy because on rainy days more people catch cabs to avoid getting wet.

What the study found, however, was something different. The actual cause was due to taxi drivers having a daily income target; due to the increased number of fares from the increase in patronage on rainy days, the cab drivers reached their daily target sooner than usual and went home early. They were ignoring the opportunity to make considerably more than their daily target.

Fixed strategies and plans have a tendency to do that: working towards fixed expectations makes you blind (to both opportunities and dangers).

Compliant but over-complicated

Head of the BCG's Institute for Organisation Yves Morieux is an ardent critic of traditional old world organisational structures. He posits that their hierarchical structure is the main contributor to the global decline in productivity over the last 50 years.

In his 2015 TED talk in London, he took particular aim at what he refers to as an organisational overreliance on 'the holy trinity of efficiency: clarity, measurement, and accountability', suggesting 'they make human effort derail'.

Morieux argues that organisational design has inadvertently led people to focus only on their own individual performance metrics, rather than collective, collaborative organisational outcomes. He claims 'we are creating organisations to fail, but in a compliant way'. Based on this notion that organisations have become failure-focussed and obsessed about the easy identification and attribution of blame, he says

> We will know who to blame, but we will never win the race … if you think about it, we pay more attention on knowing who to blame, in case we fail, than in creating the conditions to succeed.

At the crux of Morieux's argument is this: traditional organisations' emphasis on clarity, measurement and accountability as key metrics and drivers of performance were fine for the old world order; but in today's new world order of ever-increasing complexity, those metrics only serve to encourage and compound business failure.

Morieux observes that the default response of most organisations to problems associated with increased complexity is to focus even further on clarity, measurement, and accountability, and to create further, and more complicated, structures, systems and processes.

In other words, they do more of what has been done in the past, and when that doesn't work, they do even more of the same thing. The great English philosopher Alan Watts would describe this as 'all retch and no vomit'.

Morieux notes that since 1955, business complexity (as measured by the number of requirements companies are required by legislation to fulfil) has increased (at a steady rate) by a factor of six, whereas organisational complexity, in response to this, has increased by a factor of 35. In other words, organisations have completely overreacted.

To address each new legislative requirement, organisations have added more and more layers of bureaucracy, policy and systems, thereby creating greater and greater inefficiencies. As Morieux goes on to explain, many of these metrics tend to inadvertently cause negative internal competition within the business, such as for cost savings over product quality.

If this hasn't already made you want to sweep all the papers off your desk in one fell swoop—just wait. There's more.

In 2011, BCG created an 'index of complicatedness' that was based on surveys of more than 100 US and European listed companies. The index shows that over the past 15 years, the number of 'procedures, vertical layers, interface structures, coordination bodies, and decision approvals' needed in said firms had increased between 50 per cent and a staggering 350 per cent!

On average, organisations today set themselves six times as many key performance requirements as they did in 1955 (back then, CEOs were committing to four to seven performance metrics, whereas today that level has escalated to between 25 and 40).

Managers in the 20 per cent of organisations that are the most complicated by unnecessary bureaucratic layers and structures spend 40 per cent of their time report-writing, and between 30 and 60 per cent of their time in meetings. As a result, employees of these organisations were found to be three times more likely to be disengaged than employees of less bureaucratic and reactive organisations.

Linear strategy and linear structure gives us these inefficiencies. They also burden us and mean we become *slow* and *heavy*.

Linearity

Overly prescriptive and linear strategies and plans are not only untenable in a world of exponential change; they will be hugely detrimental, and not just in terms of monetary loss. Organisational survival is at stake here.

Another ardent critic of traditional organisational structures is Salim Ismail, a former vice president at Yahoo and cofounder of the Singularity University. In his book *Exponential Organizations*, Ismail suggests that 'linear product development remains the predominant name of the game...whether you are making locomotives or iPhone apps'. He says

> When you think linearly, when your operations are linear, and when your measures of performance and success are linear, you cannot help but end up with a linear organization, one that sees the world through a linear lens.

During the period of the 'Great Moderation' (the term for the period from the mid 1980s to 2008, referring to the decrease in macroeconomic volatility, predominantly in the US), large organisations have (in an effort to gain economies of scale, and increase growth and, in many cases, returns to shareholders) become even larger through acquisitions and mergers. This has led to even larger organisations becoming increasingly linear in their thinking and becoming even more inefficient due to their increased layers of bureaucracy and complexity.

What was their greatest strength (their sheer size and power) in the old world has now become their greatest weakness in the new world.

They are cumbersome, slow and above all reluctant to respond to both external and internal circumstances and pressures. Old world organisations:

- have a hierarchical structure
- are reliant upon infrastructure
- are resilient and robust
- focus on strategy and are backward-looking
- are rigid and inflexible
- are risk averse
- control their own assets
- try to make the external world fit their internal world
- focus on goals
- think linearly and sequentially
- are financially driven and interested in quantity
- aim to be the best
- are led by alpha figures
- have large numbers of employees
- prefer the status quo
- have a state of mind of dissonance and entropy.

Here lies the crux of the problem for these organisations: the landscape has changed and they are not able or willing to adapt. They may not even understand they need to.

Linear vs. exponential progress

Cofounder of PayPal Peter Thiel says in his irreverent manifesto *Zero to One*, '…today's "best practices" lead to dead ends; the best paths are new and untried'.

Thiel's core idea is that most of today's organisations have become successful by copying existing products, and making them just a little bit better. He describes this process as taking the world from '1 to *n*'; in other words, simply adding more of something we're already familiar with. According to Thiel, this type of progress is horizontal and easy to imagine, because we already know what it looks like.

In other words: it's linear. He gives as an example the typewriter: build another 100 in different colours and each with minor improvements, and you've made linear progress. Something a bit better, but not by much.

If, on the other hand, you had a typewriter, and from the bones of that typewriter you built a word processor, you have achieved vertical progress. Creating something entirely new, something fresh and unique, is what Thiel describes as a move from 0 to 1.

In other words: it's exponential. Figure 4.2 shows the difference.

Figure 4.2: zero to *n*, and zero to one

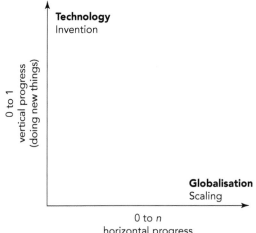

Source: *Zero to One* by Peter Thiel.

A temporary fix

The stalwarts of traditional management thinking are *finally* starting to recognise the changing times. In his 2012 *Harvard Business Review* article 'Accelerate', John Kotter acknowledges that

> the hierarchical structures and organizational processes we have used for decades to run and improve our enterprises are no longer up to the task of winning in this faster-moving world.

His solution is that firms should, in addition to their existing organisation, create and use

> a second operating system devoted to the design and implementation of strategy, that uses an agile, network like structure and a very different set of processes... [which] continually assesses the business, the industry, and the organization, and reacts with greater agility, speed and creativity than the existing one.

It must be recognised that this 'solution' is only of a temporary nature—a Band-Aid fix, if you will. Realistically, this solution could prove incredibly expensive and create inefficiencies of management the likes of which Morieux was talking about. And it doesn't answer the question of developing an ongoing understanding of the nature of change.

It should also be pointed out that Kotter's idea is nothing new; Clayton Christensen, the world's leading academic on innovation, identified a similar solution back in the late 1990s.

According to Christensen, two of the three main ways in which organisations dealing with disruption can respond are to spin out an independent organisation from the original one to develop new processes and opportunities, or to acquire new organisations that are already taking advantage of the opportunities presented in the VUCA landscape.

Of course, if either of these options were pursued, it would take incredible restraint from the 'mother' organisation not to over-manage and control its offspring; and this is something that large organisations do not have a very good track record with. (I used to work for one.)

Which leaves Christensen's last suggestion: completely restructure the organisation.

The leadership cult

The 'leadership industry' is itself showing the symptoms of the disease it claims to be trying to cure organisations of: complacency and a reliance upon old, outdated ways of thinking and doing.

Think of it in these terms. A leader for the new world order needs to be like an alpinist, who is always ready to launch the next climbing mission. Alpinists have a perpetual sense of restlessness and curiosity about themselves and the natural world. So they stay fit, both physically and mentally. They don't sit back and rest on past achievements.

Unfortunately, however, the leadership development industry has become somewhat bloated—annual global investment in the industry is estimated to be in the order of $200 *billion*—and too invested in maintaining the status quo it helped create. Rather ironically, it has not adapted to the new VUCA world.

So if you find yourself signed up to an old world leadership-development course that aims to 'empower' you to learn 'personal mastery' and your 'leadership style', and to help you 'build high-performance teams', run away in the opposite direction, and run *fast*.

We need to look to other areas for newer and fresher ideas, because what we currently have has proven to be patently ineffective and a waste of large sums of money when the environment is volatile, uncertain, complex and ambiguous.

This is not to say that the development of people is a waste of time per se (it's actually incredibly important, and indeed it's the foundation of the Alpine Style Model you'll come across in the final third of this book); it's just that you want to be sure that whoever helps you with this understands how different the new world order will be.

Because the reality of the new world order is that the most important asset of any organisation will be its people. And that's what we'll look at in the next chapter.

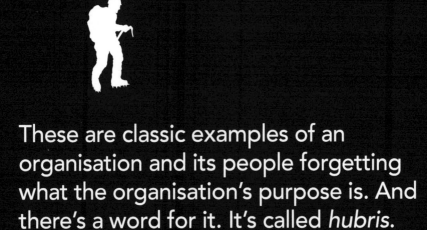

These are classic examples of an organisation and its people forgetting what the organisation's purpose is. And there's a word for it. It's called *hubris*.

CHAPTER 5

It's about people

In this chapter we'll discuss people, the most important component of any organisation, including:
- how successful organisations treat people
- the importance of people to organisations
- the three types of employees and how they affect your organisation.

If you're just about ready to give up on the traditional old world organisation and consign it to the scrapheap, you'll be pleased to know that beyond the superficial fix we discuss in chapter 4, there is hope. Fortunately, some of the guys who run these big businesses do get it. In encouraging signs, some are showing an understanding about the importance of embracing the change that VUCA brings, and being open to the new opportunities for learning. Most importantly, they have realised the crucial role that their *people* play in the new VUCA world.

One such example is Marc Bolland, CEO of major British multinational retailer Marks & Spencer (employer of approximately 80 000 people). Despite the business being 130 years old, in a radical shift for such a traditional organisation, Bolland commissioned innovative leadership and engagement firm Cirrus to develop an ongoing transformational initiative for the organisation (and I was fortunate enough to be involved with it). The initiative involved senior staff spending significant time with unconventional new world businesses like Apple, Airbnb and Uber (no old world 'personal mastery' or 'leadership styles' there, thank you). Launching the program to his staff, Bolland encouraged his senior staff to take the lead without the need for permission, to work freely and to be rebels. He encouraged them to try new things, and only asked that if they failed, they took learnings from the failure.

A quite refreshing perspective, I reckon.

An organisation of *people*

So by this point in time we've been discussing the organisation quite extensively, but if you were to ask 100 different people for their definition of a successful organisation, chances are you would get 100 different answers. To be able to build or transform to a new world organisation, it's actually pretty important to make sure your understanding is correct. Academics Ian MacDonald, Catherine Burke and Karl Stewart's book *Systems Leadership: Creating Positive Organisations* defines a *positive and successful organisation* as one that:

- achieves its purpose
- assigns workloads appropriate to and challenging for employees' capabilities
- recognises and rewards employees' work
- contributes positively to the greater society.

For the purposes of this book, this is the definition we will be following. Sure, it's not that sexy but, to put it simply, it's the best one out there by a long shot.

You'll notice that the first three points are inwardly focussed; that is, they are about the people who belong to the organisation, whether they are owners, employees or members. The points embody the equal importance of having and accomplishing a purpose that meets the expectations of the owners and members, and providing the people employed by the organisation with work that is stimulating and rewarding.

The fourth point is outwardly orientated, and focusses on the organisation's customers and broader society. Herein lies the fundamental *duality* of organisations, and it's essential that we all recognise and understand this. They have two responsibilities: firstly to serve the people who work within the organisation, and secondly to serve people who are outside of it (the customers of the organisation, and the wider society).

While there is a duality here, there is also one common trait that all four of these points share. They're all about *people*.

Why is this important?

Because organisations should serve people, not the other way round.

The entire purpose of any organisation should be to serve people: both those *within* it and those *outside* of it. It's a pretty straightforward concept, but it gets lost in organisational translation all the time.

I'm sure you can easily think of examples of interactions you've had with organisations (think of those financed by your tax dollars) where you are left feeling you have become a slave to them, and that your interaction with them is of the utmost inconvenience.

These are classic examples of an organisation and its people forgetting what the organisation's purpose is. And there's a word for it. It's called *hubris*.

Former senior executive at Royal Dutch Shell Arie de Geus remarks in his *Harvard Business Review* article 'The Living Company' that the reason many companies fail is because managers focus exclusively on producing goods and services, and forget that the organisation is a community of human beings.

Now to some people this kind of soft sentiment about the importance of people in organisations, particularly commercial ones, is entirely misplaced: after all, the primary responsibility of any commercial organisation should be to return money to the shareholder, right?

I think this is a fundamentally flawed belief.

Time and time again, organisations make the mistake of putting profits before people, but it never works. Let's look at the evidence that supports this.

The state of engagement

Gallup regularly surveys workforce engagement, even to the extent of providing a monthly figure for US employee engagement. And since early 2012, employee engagement has flatlined at about 30 per cent.

What does this mean?

Gallup defines an engaged worker as one who is 'involved in, enthusiastic about and committed to their work and workplace'—in other words, this is someone who when asked about their job says 'Yep, it's a good job, I enjoy it'. But that's only a third of the story. An alarming *50 per cent* of US employees are disengaged with their work—this would sound something like 'Well, it pays the bills, but I'd rather be doing something else'—and another 20 per cent are *actively* disengaged with their work—this would sound something like 'I *hate* this job, and I *hate* this organisation'.

The estimated annual cost to the US economy of employee disengagement is $500 billion.

And Gallup doesn't only focus on the American workplace. In what *Forbes* magazine described as the 'Mother of All Employee Engagement Surveys', in 2013 Gallup released the results of its global workplace study across 142 countries. The results are presented in table 5.1.

Table 5.1: employee engagement levels

Country/Region	Engaged (%)	Disengaged (%)	Actively disengaged (%)
Australia	25	60	15
South East Asia	12	73	14
USA	30	50	20
Western Europe	14	66	20

As you can see, and what should concern us all, is that the poor numbers for the US are actually the *best* in the world.

The Australian results are slightly worse (with a predicted annual cost to the Australian economy of $50 billion), but what about engagement levels elsewhere, particularly in Western Europe and South East Asia? This is scary, scary stuff.

There are countless additional surveys, academic papers and anecdotes that consistently confirm the sentiment of Gallup's engagement surveys.

It's the first part of the perfect storm. *People.* In the VUCA world, we have to see people as valuable, and to give them opportunities for *meaningful* work. Author Daniel Pink in his book *Drive: The surprising truth about what motivates us* talks about the three vital ingredients that comprise motivation: autonomy, mastery and purpose. He argues that having autonomy (the choice to decide how to do the work) and mastery (the opportunity to master the work) are important to driving motivation, but more than anything, it's about the work having purpose (the opportunity to do work that is meaningful).

Part of this is making sure that people are engaged in the workplace—and providing the opportunity for meaningful work—but another part of this is about trust. Remembering that organisations are ultimately about people, both inside and outside of the organisation, having trust between the people and the organisation is crucial.

Who do you trust?

But what happens if trust is absent?

We'll return to the issue of employee engagement in a little bit, but first let's look into what may be one of the causes of this disengagement: a widespread lack of trust. For the past 15 years the independent public relations firm Edelman has annually tracked levels of trust in the global institutions of business, government, media and non-government organisations. Like Gallup's employee engagement numbers, the results of the 2015 Edelman Trust Barometer are just a little startling.

While they acknowledge that there are always long cyclical changes in institutional trust, never had they recorded such a dramatic decrease as they did in 2014. Across the board, in business, government, media and non-government organisations, global trust fell or, as Edelman described it, 'evaporated'.

The survey is based on the sampling of informed populations from 27 developed and developing nations, and in 2015 the number of trusting people fell to an all-time low. Only six out of 27 countries had organisational trust levels above 60 per cent. Distrust of the media sector was found in two-thirds of the countries surveyed. Public confidence in business CEOs has absolutely fallen off a cliff: in the developed world, 70 per cent of respondents did not perceive CEOs to be a believable source of information. (The only category that ranks lower: government spokespeople.)

North Americans in particular have had their trust in organisations tested over the past decade and a half. The staggering deception of Enron's executive team laid the foundation for this mistrust in 2001, and it only grew deeper after the GFC of 2008, especially when the appalling self-interest of the ratings agencies and the banks that created the mess became apparent. Add to this the game of chicken played between President Obama and the US Congress in 2012 and 2013. It's understandable that people's patience is being tested.

Even today, as the wealth gap between the richest and the poorest becomes increasingly larger on a global scale, there is considerable distrust and ill feeling towards large organisations. Understandable, when in some developed countries the pay gap between the average CEO and non-skilled workers is at a ratio of 350:1.

As Charles-Édouard Bouée describes in *Light Footprint Management*:

> ...when people have lost their faith in the competence of their leaders...when our politicians squabble, while living standards fall; when our companies are seen to have been hijacked by a predatory, amoral elite bent on their own enrichment at the expense of employees, savers and pensioners; and when our institutions seem out-dated and incapable of managing our economies and societies at a time of unprecedented turbulence and uncertainty, there is a hunger for a new deal.

The question that you must ask yourself is: Do you want to be part of Bouée's 'new deal'? Do you want to be part of a successful organisation, enriching the lives of those who work for it and of those it serves? Or would you rather belong to an organisation that takes from rather than gives to society, and contributes to these high employee disengagement and public distrust numbers?

These are the two options you have going into the new VUCA world. Make sure you choose wisely.

Disengaged and destructive

As we saw previously, an alarmingly large proportion of workers across the globe (70 per cent) are currently disengaged or actively disengaged (aka destructive) in the work they do on a daily basis. Let's look at these people in a bit more detail.

Disengaged

A typically disengaged worker is sleepwalking through their daily work and, despite being physically present, is mentally absent and has little, if any, motivation and energy. As noted previously, if asked about their job, this person is likely to respond that 'it pays the bills' and nothing more.

Whether it's an individual or a team or an organisation of disengaged people, they will be either unaware of or complacent about the coming change.

In the face of VUCA, this individual (or team, or organisation) will stick their head in the sand and ignore the realities ahead. If asked whether they are prepared to get uncomfortable in confronting and adapting to VUCA, the collective response would likely be 'what change?' or simply 'no thanks'.

What is the one thing that is consistent with disengaged teams? A lack of purpose. Articulate a purpose that resonates both logically and emotionally for team members, and the engagement will follow. Not only that, but it will make the hard work much easier to do.

Destructive

A destructive person (identified by Gallup as being 'actively disengaged') not only has no desire or passion for the work they do, they *actively* display their disengagement and contempt. The self-perception of this person is that it is not their fault they are in the job that they are in, and they seek to undermine not only the work of their fellow team members but also of the organisation as a whole. This person is likely to tell anybody who will listen that 'I HATE this job'.

Whether it's an individual or a team or an organisation of destructive workers, you'll find them to be highly reactive to and feel threatened by the uncertainty that VUCA brings.

Not only will they deny the reality, they'll seek to fight it.

As difficult as this may sound, the goal of any organisation should be to rid themselves of these disengaged workers (*especially* the destructive ones). These workers are the cancer that will slowly undermine and destroy the organisation's culture from within and completely remove the possibility for organisational adaptation to VUCA.

Engaged and beyond

What about the smaller proportion of people that Gallup *has* identified as being engaged with their work? These are the people who need to become the foundation for your transition into the new VUCA world.

We actually need to further categorise this group of engaged workers to really understand what an asset they can be to an organisation operating in uncertain conditions.

Engaged

Simply put, engaged workers enjoy the work that they do. They feel a connection to the organisation's purpose, and are prepared to put in extra effort if needed. As we saw previously, if asked about their work, they're likely to say 'Yep, it's a good job, I enjoy it'.

Whether it's an individual or a team or an organisation of engaged workers, you'll find they are collegiate with one another, and accepting of the VUCA landscape. They know it will throw multiple challenges at them, but they are okay with that. When asked if they are prepared to get uncomfortable in confronting VUCA, the collective response of the group would be along the lines of 'Of course'.

The goal of any organisation should be to normalise these people. Not only should they be the bedrock upon which the organisation is built, they are the foundation from which *inspired* and *destined* workers can grow. They are solid, reliable workers who care about their work and the future of the organisation. Any potential new employees who don't show this basic level of commitment and passion shouldn't make it through the door.

Inspired

An inspired worker is more than just engaged; they are passionate and energised. They are comfortable with the notion of being uncomfortable, and accept that it goes with the terrain. When asked about their work, they are likely to say 'I LOVE my job'. Whether it's an individual or a team or an organisation of inspired workers, they'll be comfortable with the challenges of the VUCA world. 'Yes,' they say, 'bring it on!'

Destined

A destined worker truly feels as if they were born to do the work they're doing. They are completely committed; the work is their 'calling'. They often find the work challenging, but they love to be challenged. In fact, they seek it out whenever they can. A destined worker will go out of their way to tell others 'I was BORN for this job'. Whether it's an individual or a team or an organisation of destined workers, they're going to achieve big things, or if they don't, they'll go down fighting. They will approach the VUCA world with an appetite for the challenge and a hunger and curiosity for what lies ahead. Not only will they say 'Yes' to the challenge, they will say 'What else is out there?'

They will want to know what other mountains are out there for them to climb.

Not surprisingly, the goal of any organisation should be to maximise and celebrate these people. These people form special teams that become a force to be reckoned with. Their mantra becomes: 'Who dares, wins'. They are the luminaries all other employees within the organisation should aspire to be.

These are the people who, if not already there, are willing to become alpinists. They are ready to move light and fast to reach the summit. These are the people who want to embrace change and understand it, and see VUCA not as terrifying, but as an opportunity for a future we could never have imagined.

This brings us to the end of part I. In part II, we learn about expedition-style organisations and alpine-style organisations, and how to transition from expedition style (which may have served you well in the old world) to alpine style (the only way to survive and thrive in the VUCA world). Read on!

The approaches

Traditional organisations aim for the summit, complete with harpoon and cannon.

CHAPTER 6

All that is wrong with expedition style

In this chapter we'll learn about the expedition-style approach to mountaineering and business, including:
- **how the Everest disaster of 1996 illustrates the flaws of expedition style**
- **what the business world learned from that disaster**
- **how expedition-style mountaineering came to be**
- **the characteristics of expedition-style organisations.**

In May 1996, the world's most infamous mountaineering disaster occurred on Mount Everest. While it was not the world's *greatest* mountaineering disaster (there have been numerous events on Everest and other mountains in the Himalaya with much greater loss of life, most recently in 2014 and 2015), the 1996 events on Everest were definitely the most *publicised* of any disaster or accident in the history of mountaineering.

But you could be forgiven for thinking it was the greatest mountaineering disaster to have happened—the entire understanding of mountaineering for most laypeople is derived purely from what they have read, seen or heard about these events.

At last count, literally hundreds of newspaper and magazine articles, in addition to 11 books, one genuinely excellent IMAX documentary, one (surprisingly) very good 3D Hollywood blockbuster, a truly terrible made-for-TV movie, two TV documentaries and a pop song ('The Climber', by Kiwi songwriter Neil Finn) have focused on, or, in the case of the song been 'inspired by', these events on Everest.

Nearly two decades after the disaster, it still captures people's imagination.

Why is this the case? Let's have a look.

High-altitude organisations

In the early 1990s, commercial mountaineering in the Himalaya had started to take off. Commercial mountaineering is where, rather than an expedition consisting of friends climbing for pleasure, or of national representatives climbing for country, the expedition is organised by a commercial organisation looking for profit. Paying clients, generally with a varying climbing background (ranging from some experience to absolutely none) are led up the mountain by experienced professional guides. (As the examples in chapter 2 illustrate, in the Himalaya it's an effective but arguably risky way of climbing a mountain, because it involves outsourcing skill development, decision making and risk management to someone else.)

New Zealand mountaineering guide Rob Hall had started a business guiding the 'Seven Summits', the highest mountains on each of the seven continents, of which Mount Everest is the most difficult and the tallest. (Everest, standing at 8850 metres, is nearly 9 vertical kilometres above sea level, and is the highest peak in both Asia and the world).

Over a six-year period, Hall and his company, Adventure Consultants, had successfully guided 39 paying clients to the summit of Everest, with Hall going as far as to say that he had Everest 'all figured out' and had built a 'yellow brick road to the summit'.

Having seen Hall's success, naturally enough, other ambitious climbers were keen for a piece of the Sherpa-assisted pie, including Hall's American friend and occasional climbing partner, Scott Fischer. Subsequently, Fischer launched his own commercial guiding service, called Mountain Madness.

The climbing season of 1996 was the first time both Hall's and Fischer's businesses were operating on Mount Everest at the same time, with both parties intending to climb to the summit via the relatively non-technical (but still not easy) south-east ridge. Despite their friendship, their businesses would effectively be in direct competition on the mountain. The stakes were raised when both businesses began vying to have experienced mountaineer and journalist Jon Krakauer on board: the exposure for the business that hosted him—an article in the widely read publication *Outside* magazine—would be incredible publicity.

Hall eventually won the competition; Krakauer joined the Adventure Consultants team.

As somewhat of a consolation prize New York socialite Sandy Hill Pittman (at the time married to Bob Pittman, the incredibly wealthy cofounder of MTV) joined the Mountain Madness team, and planned to send live dispatches from the mountain to American media giant NBC, via a primitive and very heavy satellite phone (that Pittman's Sherpa guide, Lopsang Jangbu Sherpa, carried).

Given the worldwide exposure, there was an incredible amount at stake for both Hall and Fischer. They needed to prove both their reputations and their businesses. For the first time ever, Himalayan mountaineering was about to be broadcast in real time to the whole world. (Interestingly, it was an early premonition of the changing world where people, places and technology interact to create previously unimaginable circumstances.)

By early May, and with considerable support from the often underappreciated Sherpa climbers who do most of the heavy load carries, the teams had laboured on the mountain for five weeks, and were ready for their final summit push. In a somewhat alarming indicator of a very fixed mindset, Hall had earlier stated his intention to summit on 10 May, a date that had been lucky for him on Everest in the past. Just before midnight on the night of 9 May 1996, a total of 34 climbers (members from Hall's, Fischer's, and several other teams also on Everest) left their tents at Camp 4, at an altitude of just under 8000 metres, and headed for the summit. The round trip includes 850 vertical metres of climbing and descending and normally takes between 16 and 24 hours to complete.

In addition to the inherent difficulties associated with climbing slopes of rock and snow in temperatures of –30 degrees Celsius, climbing this high up in the earth's atmosphere is nearly impossible due to incredibly low levels of atmospheric pressure. This results in limited oxygen availability (about 25 per cent of what is available at sea level—if you were transported instantaneously up to the summit from sea level, you would die within a matter of minutes from oxygen deprivation).

Thus, the final stage of the climb is *extremely* dangerous. Due to the varying skill and fitness levels within the teams, the climbers progressed at different speeds and the faster climbers often had to sit down and wait—in literally freezing conditions—for periods of up to two hours for the slower members to catch up.

By late morning of 10 May, the climbers were spread out across the final summit ridge, at a height of 8800 metres above sea level. The snow-laden ridge is incredibly narrow, with drops of 2500 and 3000 metres on either side. At one point on the ridge you *literally* have 3 kilometres of air beneath your feet. It's pretty crazy up there.

On final summit pushes on Everest, turnaround times are set to ensure that climbers have enough time to make it back to their tents before nightfall. Most teams set their turnaround time as midday, although in recent years the trend has been for earlier times of 10 and 11 am (as improvements in training techniques, equipment and oxygen apparatus seem to be making ascent times a little quicker).

If the climber is not literally within an arm's reach of the summit by the turnaround time, the rule says they must turn around and start their descent immediately. If you're not back in your tent at Camp 4 by nightfall, it means you will have been on the move in an incredibly cold and low-oxygen environment for 24 hours straight. You will be fatigued beyond comprehension, your oxygen will have run out and you will be near death.

And this is what turned out to be one of the biggest mistakes made on 10 May 1996—only a very vague turnaround time of either 1 or 2 pm had been identified by both Hall and Fischer, and, perhaps due to this vagueness, climbers from both parties ignored it. With the first climbers summiting just after 1 pm and continuing to do so until late in the day, it was seemingly inevitable that something would go wrong.

By the late afternoon of 10 May, a not-uncommon storm had arrived on the mountain, causing many of the already exhausted climbers to become lost in hazardous conditions on their descent. The storm blew throughout the night and many of the climbers did not make it back to their tents at Camp 4.

By the next afternoon, eight climbers, including Hall and Fischer, two of the world's best high-altitude mountaineers at that time, had lost their lives in the storm. And by the end of the 1996 Everest climbing season, only a few weeks later, another five lives had been lost.

In total, in the space of a few weeks, 13 climbers had lost their lives and, in a macabre fashion, due to emergent satellite phone technology and Pittman's daily updates to NBC, the events played out in front of the world's media. The global media coverage reached a crescendo in September 1996 when Krakauer's account of the climb was published in *Outside*, and then again in 1997 when Krakauer went on to write his bestselling book describing the events, *Into Thin Air: A Personal Account of the Everest Disaster.*

Given the Shakespearian combination of drama and tragedy, combined with the global media coverage, it is not surprising that the events of 1996 have become ingrained in mountaineering folklore.

Mountaineering and MBAs?

But what *is* surprising and indeed somewhat peculiar, is that the disaster has become a widely examined case study at business schools around the world; MBA students are required to dissect the events and conduct SWOT analyses and deliver presentations about what they have learned.

Seriously? WTF?!

Yes, seriously. It's been picked over by various academics and, at last count, one business book and five academic papers have been written about the events of 1996. Three of these papers have even been published by the esteemed business journal the *Harvard Business Review.*

At least two American business professors who authored case studies on the events have built successful consulting practices based, in part, on their analysis of what happened, and one has co-developed (with Harvard Business School) a computer-based simulation of an expedition to Mount Everest, jarringly complete with climbers that slide up and down the mountain in a fashion not too dissimilar to the cliffhanger game on TV game show *The Price Is Right* (thankfully sans yodelling).

If the future leaders of our organisations are currently completing MBAs where they learn how to run the businesses of tomorrow by using tools like this, then Houston, *we have a problem.*

Perhaps the most interesting and relevant academic studies of all were two that looked not specifically at the events of Mount Everest in 1996, but rather at all records of Himalayan climbing expeditions over a period of decades. The studies, undertaken by Eric Anicich and Adam Galinsky from the Columbia Business School and Roderick Swaab from INSEAD's Department of Organisational Behaviour, surveyed 21 'highly experienced' climbers from 27 countries, then analysed the records of the Himalayan Database, which has documented the activities of 30 625 climbers from 56 countries on 5104 expeditions.

The studies found expedition teams from countries with hierarchical cultures were more likely to reach the summit, but were also more likely to have climbers killed along the way.

Slightly sensationalist findings aside, the analyses are not particularly surprising. Harvard Business School professor Michael Roberto reports in his two Everest papers that

- cognitive biases
- questionable team beliefs about interpersonal risk-taking
- system complexity

all interacted to contribute towards the disaster.

Wharton Business School professor Michael Useem identified an inability for people to manage 'up' the hierarchical structure of the teams as a key cause.

George Washington University professor Christopher Kayes in his book *Destructive Goal Pursuit: The Mount Everest Disaster* identified the concept of 'goalodicy', which he describes as:

> a situation in which the normally helpful process of goal-setting becomes dysfunctional; the effort put toward achieving a goal results in unintended consequences, such as breakdowns in teamwork and learning, unethical decisions, excessive risk-taking, difficulty in abandoning the goal even when the signs point to failure, and finally, an inability to actually achieve the goal.

As Kayes says, the value of goal setting has become ingrained in the culture of our organisations, and 'goals have become the theology of contemporary leadership'.

Looking at the events of 1996, however, Kayes argued the setting and pursuing of audacious goals often drives failure.

Kayes's theory is that the more the climbers focussed on their goal—standing on the summit of Mount Everest—the more the goal grew beyond just an external endpoint they were working towards, and became a part of their own identity and sense of self-worth.

Kayes also notes from another, earlier study on Everest mountaineers attempting a difficult, never-before-climbed route on the west face: 'the more uncertain climbers felt about their possible success in reaching the summit, the more likely they were to invest in their particular strategy'. Kayes notes that as the uncertainty and risks of the climb mounted, not only did their plan become threatened, but so too did their identities. Their commitment to their goal had become part of their identity.

Ironically, the uncertainty only served to further their investment in a plan that was looking increasingly dangerous.

All of these studies are very good, and very interesting. However, they're not particularly useful for the new VUCA world. They only serve to tell us what *not* to do in organisations, and for the most part only confirm what we already know.

None of them provide any new insight into what organisations can do to get better, and how they can adapt to and manage a complex and uncertain world.

The wrong type of mountaineering

The problem is this. These studies are looking at the *wrong type* of mountaineering. Learning from the events of Mount Everest in 1996 is about as useful for organisations in today's VUCA world as it would be to learn how to drive a Tesla car from shovelling coal in an American steam train from the 1850s.

There are two reasons for this.

Firstly, the climbers in those teams on Everest were no more teammates than are the passengers of Flight QF 10 on the daily transpacific flight from Sydney to Los Angeles. Despite having the same end-goal of getting to their destination (whether that is the summit of Everest or the taxi rank at LAX), they are not team members in the sense we apply to work and organisations.

This is the reality of most modern-day commercial mountaineering expeditions: adventure tourists (or passengers posing as team members) are in it only for themselves. The success of others is irrelevant.

There is little, if any, relevance for organisations in the new world, which is about adapting to change rather than just stubbornly ignoring it.

Secondly, and even more importantly — indeed, the entire crux of the book is based on this idea — the climbing approach employed by commercial expeditions, known as *expedition-style*, also has very little relevance to organisations working in the new world order. Lessons from expedition-style mountaineering did have relevance to the organisations of the old world order, where status quo was the norm, and where rigid structure, control, and a dependence upon infrastructure could be used to overcome challenges (as long as they sat within certain accepted bounds). There is, however, no relevance to organisations in the new world order, where uncertainty and complexity are the norm.

The traditional expedition-style approach to climbing a mountain is as outdated as the traditional, linear, hierarchical structure of the organisation. To understand why this is the case, we need to understand a bit more about the expedition-style approach, followed by its newer alternative.

The origin of expedition style

The expedition-style approach to mountaineering has its roots in the Himalaya, the highest mountain range on earth. It is home to all 14 of the '8000ers' (so-called because these mountains are higher than 8000 metres in altitude, and were initially considered by many to be unclimbable due to the very low levels of oxygen at their summits). It was only in the aftermath of World War II, when the war-weary nations of Europe and North America were looking to reassert their national pride, that these previously unclimbed mountains were targeted and climbed.

In the space of only 14 years, from 1950 to 1964, all 14 of these 8000ers were climbed, including of course Mount Everest, which was climbed by the British expedition in 1953—although the successful summit team consisted of Nepali Tenzing Norgay and New Zealander Edmund Hillary. (What few people know is that only a year earlier a Swiss team, including Norgay, had pioneered the route subsequently used by the British, and got to within 250 metres of the summit.)

Due to the remoteness of the Himalaya, and the extreme altitudes and associated cold temperatures and lack of oxygen on the 8000ers, expeditions to climb them were initially lengthy and cumbersome affairs (and for the most part they still are today). They took many months to complete and involved literally hundreds of climbers and support staff.

For example, the British Mount Everest Expedition in 1953 was conducted very much like a military campaign; it was led by the British Army's Colonel John Hunt, and took five months to complete. The total expedition party comprised approximately 400 people, with seven camps placed on the mountain, and it was only at the end of the fourth month that they were ready to make their summit push.

Large amounts of equipment, ropes and oxygen bottles were used to overcome the difficulties of the extreme altitude and cold (all up, in excess of 13 tons of equipment was carried to Base

Camp). As an example of the expedition's focus on summiting at all costs (rather than on the style in which they did it), at one point they considered a proposal to use both a cannon and harpoon on their mission—the former as a means to deter avalanche ('it worked in the Alps', records Hunt in his journal) and the latter to '…fire a grapnel from the South Col to the summit'. As veteran alpinist Mark Twight describes it, this type of climbing lays 'a veritable siege of the mountain'.

It's a style that involves lots of people, lots of equipment, lots of energy and lots of time to overpower the challenges of the mountain.

Expedition-style climbing means the use of multiple pre-stocked camps on the way to the summit, with fixed ropes installed on the mountain to lead climbers up and down the route. It has in the past two decades become vastly popular with commercial expeditions, because it allows for less experienced climbers to be involved in expeditions from which they would otherwise be precluded. Other than Everest, another good example of a popular modern expedition-style climb is the West Buttress of Denali (formerly called Mount McKinley).

Expedition-style climbing is still the most dominant style of mountaineering today, particularly in the world's highest mountain ranges and especially in the Himalaya. It has spawned a multimillion-dollar commercial climbing industry, where thousands of relatively inexperienced climbers now annually travel to the Himalaya to be guided up the world's highest mountains by experienced Western and Sherpa guides. More than 90 per cent of climbs undertaken in Nepal, the epicentre of Himalayan climbing, are done in expedition style.

By its nature, it is obvious that expedition-style mountaineering is, in organisational terms, hierarchical and belonging to the old world order.

And, as we identify in chapter 2, it does work, *when* the weather cooperates and things go to plan. This can still be seen to this day on Mount Everest, where during the annual climbing season up to 300 people and beyond are summiting. By a process of sheer weight of numbers and manpower, with up to 30 commercial expeditions, each consisting of a group of paying clients and Western guides (up to 30 for the larger expeditions) and supporting Sherpa climbers (up to 40 for the larger expeditions) gathering on the Nepali side every northern hemisphere spring, expedition style *overwhelms* the mountain. With infrastructure provided on the mountain, it is not uncommon now to encounter climbers on Everest with big dreams but with no previous mountaineering experience whatsoever. (I wouldn't have believed this myself, had I not come across multiple climbers fitting this description on Everest in 2010.)

Expedition style enables climbers deep in the pocket but light on skills a reasonable shot at summiting, if they have got themselves fit enough and if the weather cooperates.

This is fine of course until the unexpected happens — remember Nassim Nicholas Taleb's Black Swans? — and then everyone realises that Everest, Mother Goddess of the Earth, isn't actually as safe and stable and predictable as they have led themselves to believe.

The end result is death. Large-scale death. As chapter 2 illustrates, this was seen with the tragic loss of 16 Sherpa lives in an avalanche in 2014, and then again in 2015, with the loss of 19 people killed at Base Camp after a large earthquake caused a massive avalanche.

And for every fatality there is an untold number of close calls, near-death experiences and rescues up high that nobody will ever tell you about (it ruins their story of how they 'conquered' the mountain). Again, I wouldn't have believed this myself, had I not seen it. Don't be fooled by the stories.

A desire to control and simplify

At its core, expedition style is all about people attempting to *control* and *simplify* an environment that is naturally volatile, uncertain and complex. When things go to plan and the weather cooperates, it's a style that works. But when things go pear-shaped, as they inevitably do in a VUCA world, they go pear-shaped in a pretty major way. Actually, make that a *majorly* major way. And although expedition style, because of its size and strength and power, is resilient and robust, this is only true up until a certain point, beyond which it fails.

Today's organisations operate in a very similar fashion to that of expedition-style mountaineering—to the extent that they use the expedition-style approach for most things they do. And in the new VUCA world, when things go pear-shaped in a major way on a more regular basis, they too are prone to breaking, often in a spectacular fashion.

Traditional organisations aim for the summit, complete with harpoon and cannon.

As we read in chapter 5, our tendency has been to take a linear approach to measuring organisational performance. This applies to:

- operations
- metrics
- thinking.

The majority of our organisations are currently using a linear design, which has hardly changed in the previous 150 years. And the similarities between the expedition–style approach to climbing a mountain and the linear approach to structuring and operating an organisation are quite remarkable.

We previously discussed the characteristics of traditional linear organisations, including a top-down hierarchical structure, a tendency for strategic planning based on past history, and sequential thinking. They, like expedition-style mountaineering:

- have a hierarchical structure
- are reliant upon infrastructure
- focus on strategy
- are rigid and inflexible
- think linearly and sequentially
- are led by alpha figures.

They are resilient and they are robust, but in the VUCA world, that is not enough.

But luckily for us, there is another way.

There is a newer style of mountaineering that has enormous relevance and learning potential for organisations looking to adapt to the VUCA world.

It's called *alpine style*, and we first encountered it when we heard the story of Ueli Steck and his light and fast ascent of the Eiger in the introduction.

So what is alpine style?

It's the opposite of fragile.

The opposite of fragile

Common sense would suggest that to get ourselves ready for this onslaught of VUCA (and Black Swans) we will need to make ourselves and our organisations become the opposite of fragile.

The opposite of fragile—what would that be? Resilient? Robust, perhaps?

Not quite.

Just as the opposite of positive is negative, not neutral, the opposite of fragility is not resilience or robustness, but rather, the negative of fragility—*antifragility*. In his book *Antifragile: Things That Gain from Disorder*, Nassim Nicholas Taleb notes that this 'blind spot' is universal—there is no word in any known modern or ancient language meaning *antifragile*. Says Taleb, 'half of life—the interesting half—we don't have a name for'.

Things that are fragile break easily and generally degenerate over a period of time: think of muscle atrophy in someone who is bedridden. Not to be confused with something that is robust and resilient (i.e. something that withstands the forces of change, but in doing so does not change itself), things that are antifragile actually *get better* as a result of their exposure to disorder. They benefit from shocks, and thrive and grow when exposed to volatility, randomness and uncertainty.

In case you're wondering, alpine style is antifragile.

As Taleb says, antifragility loves randomness and uncertainty, and it allows us to deal with the unknown, even when we don't understand it. And as chapter 3 illustrates, not understanding things is going to happen to us a whole lot more in the VUCA world.

Taleb describes a spectrum, from fragility to resilience to antifragility. As we move from the old world to the new world, we can see the move to antifragility is also required.

On the left-hand side of the spectrum we have fragility: things that either suffer during or break from volatility. An empty china teacup knocked from a table is a good example. Fragility prefers tranquility, because it has more to lose than to gain during volatile times. When something fragile breaks, it does so in a catastrophic fashion.

In the middle of the spectrum lies resilience and robustness. Things that are resilient and robust always stay the same; they are resistant to change. In other words, they *never* change. Instead of an empty china teacup knocked off a table, think of a plastic cup—it doesn't break, it just bounces and neither breaks nor changes shape.

On the right-hand side of the spectrum we have antifragility. Antifragile things are beyond resilience and robustness: they actually *improve* under pressure. The antifragile teacup knocked from a table not only bounces back but returns to the table intact and brimming with freshly steeped tea.

With the best of intentions, and in the same fashion as expedition-style mountaineering teams, our organisations have been constructed with resilience and robustness in mind. Like the seawall at the Fukushima nuclear plant, they have been built with hard outer edges to withstand events and shocks of *expected* magnitude.

The perfect storm, however, will bring with it events and shocks of *unknown* magnitude. Robust structures with hard outer edges may survive the storm, but they will be left behind as relics of the old world. The new world will have moved on, and only those who are antifragile and alpine style will be able to keep up.

So, if the answer is to go light and fast and adopt an alpine-style approach, where will we start? How do we build such organisations? Well, we'll need to learn more about alpine style. That's what we'll cover in the next chapter.

Alpinists *seek* uncertainty and ambiguity.

CHAPTER 7

All that is right with alpine style

Now we get to the key to adapting to the VUCA world: alpine style. In this chapter we learn:
- of Athol Whimp and Andrew Lindblade's stunning alpine-style mountaineering feats
- about the history of alpine-style climbing
- why alpine style trumps expedition style.

Early on the morning of 14 December 1991, a large part of the east face of Mount Cook, New Zealand's highest mountain, simply fell away. An estimated 14 million cubic metres of rock gouged a 1.5-kilometre-wide path down the valley as it fell. The height of Cook was reduced by nearly 30 metres to its current altitude of 3724 metres. Already a technically difficult climb, Mount Cook instantly became even more challenging.

That is the nature of the mountains: few environments on earth are as volatile, uncertain, complex and ambiguous; they are constantly changing. But extremes of temperature and altitude are not the only differentiators of mountainous environments. The mountains that create alpine zones (at least the ones that seem to attract mountaineers) are generally relatively young, meaning they are only recently formed. As such, they have had little time to be reduced in height and jaggedness by the erosive forces of wind, snow and ice. Alpine environments are therefore highly unstable, and it is the combination of these cold temperatures, high altitudes and fierce storms with unstable geology that make them the VUCA environments they are.

Indeed, when you consider the risks that are present in the alpine environment, it might be difficult to even understand why alpinists would choose to go there in the first place. But then again, that *is* what makes an alpinist an alpinist.

Alpinists seek uncertainty and ambiguity.

They recognise the benefits of venturing into the unknown and learning about themselves, each other and the world around them.

To really get to the core of what the alpine-style approach to mountaineering is all about, we need to know what an alpine-style ascent looks, sounds and feels like. We need to get dirty.

One of the best ways that we can do this is by looking at the accomplishments of a climbing partnership that set a new global benchmark for alpine-style climbing in the 1990s and 2000s.

An enduring partnership

During this period, New Zealander Athol Whimp and Australian Andrew Lindblade redefined what was possible in the mountains with a commitment to climbing light and fast. In addition to being a highly skilled climber, Lindblade is a beautiful writer, and in his somewhat ironically titled book *Expeditions* (ironic in that Lindblade and Whimp abhorred expedition-style ascents), we gain great insight into the alpine-style approach.

For the best part of a decade, Whimp and Lindblade went on a journey of development and growth that saw them become one of the world's leading pairs of alpinists. They cut their teeth on the beautiful rock of the Arapiles and Grampians in south-eastern Australia, and then the snow and ice of New Zealand's steep, technical and weather-beaten Southern Alps, before taking their skills to the greater mountain ranges of the world. They climbed hard technical routes in Yosemite and Patagonia before eventually moving on to test their alpine-style skills in the home of expedition style, the Himalaya.

After a failed attempt in 1996 on Thalay Sagar, a notoriously difficult and cold 6904-metre mountain in the Indian Himalaya, they returned in 1997 and made a first ascent of a challenging new route on the mountain's north face. For this ascent they were awarded the 1998 Piolet D'or, the Golden Ice Axe, an annual award given by the alpine climbing fraternity to recognise the highest achievement and evolution in alpinism.

In 2000, Whimp and Lindblade set out to climb a new direct route on the unclimbed north face of Jannu, a 7710-metre mountain in the Nepali Himalaya. The north face of Jannu is a 2000-metre-high vertical wall of rock and ice, and was at that time considered by some of the world's leading climbers to be the 'last great problem in the Himalaya' (referring to the fact that the route had never been directly climbed before, despite repeated attempts, and thus the 'problem' remained unsolved).

Approximately halfway up the face on their attempt, Whimp and Lindblade were almost killed early one morning by a violent avalanche of rock and ice that tore through their portaledge (a small hanging tent designed to enable sleeping when climbing vertical walls). They were very lucky to be alive. Shaken but only mildly stirred, they composed themselves, descended to base camp, regathered from their near-death experience, and then turned their attention instead to an alternative route to the left of the north face. Known as the Wall of Shadows, this alternative route had only been climbed twice before, the first time by a Japanese party in 1976 (who climbed the route expedition style, fixing the entire route with rope), and then by a combined team of Swiss and Dutch climbers in 1987 (with two of the Dutch climbers dying on the descent).

What is most impressive about their climb is that after coming so close to losing their lives on their direct line attempt only a few days earlier, Whimp and Lindblade were able to quickly compose themselves and refocus their attention on the alternative objective. This speaks volumes about their drive, determination and resilience and their commitment to one another: most people who had survived such a violent ordeal would probably walk away from the mountains, vowing never to return.

Not Whimp and Lindblade. With the destruction of the portaledge precluding them from reattempting their original direct route, they simply got back to work and found an alternative way to climb the mountain.

Reflected in their actions was their attitude to the climb and to their surrounding environment: if the circumstances change, and the initial plan doesn't work, come up with a new plan. Don't sit around and mourn what could have been; rather, have an open mindset, keep moving and forge a new path.

This was an alpine-style ethos at its best.

Following the avalanche and their retreat, they rested in base camp for only two days before they launched up the mountain on the Wall of Shadows. Three days of difficult climbing from base camp took them to their highest tent site at 6750 metres, from where they embarked on a 48-hour round-trip to the summit and back. They were travelling in pure alpine style, leaving their tent, sleeping bags, mats and most of their climbing rack at their camp, instead carrying only one backpack between them, with its contents being a day's worth of snack food, a small stove and gas, some soup powder, one rope, and a small number of ice screws and carabiners.

They used their previous decade's worth of learning, of skill development and experience, their 10000 hours so to speak, to be able to summit in this manner. They travelled light and fast, taking as little equipment as they needed, and nothing more. They used the surrounding environment wherever possible to assist them: the stove enabled them to melt ice for water, and rather than carrying a heavy rack of climbing equipment they chose to take just three ice screws, enabling them to secure themselves to the vertical ice as they pitched upwards.

When the climbing was steep enough to warrant, they used the rope as protection from falling; when it wasn't, the rope went back in their pack, enabling them to move faster.

Unlike expedition style, there was no fixing of rope here.

They spent the night at an altitude of 7500 metres in a small crevasse. They sat on their shared backpack, forgoing the comfort of a tent, sleeping bag and mat for this lightweight approach. With the temperatures well below zero, they were uncomfortable to the extent that they didn't sleep, but that didn't matter. They were intimately engaged with their hostile surroundings, and were able to draw comfort from within themselves and from each other.

Lindblade describes Whimp speaking of a profound sense of detachment from base camp and their lives back at home. They were both simply in the moment, steadfast in their commitment to the mountain and focussed on what they had to do to get through the night, and with hope for what the morning would bring: getting to the summit and back down safely.

They reached the summit the next morning and quickly started their descent, arriving back to their tent 48 hours after they had first left it, exhausted but incredibly satisfied with their accomplishment. After their return to base camp they commenced their trek back home to civilisation and their lives in Australia, but Lindblade described being keenly aware of what they were leaving behind on Jannu:

> never before had I felt such a strong sense of communion between the cautious, rational mind, and the deeper, profound 'life force' as I did during our time on Jannu's summit ridge ... Something inside was always connected to a belief and acceptance of all; something, somewhere, absolute and pure.

This description is a very powerful evocation of someone fully engaged in the work they are doing. The language is of someone so at one with their activity that it feels like their destiny.

Alpine style in a VUCA world

Lindblade, a staunch critic of commercial expeditions, wrote an article for *Rock* magazine titled 'Overcoming the Banality of Mountaineering'. Speaking about the trend of commercialised expeditions in the Himalaya, Lindblade points out that many of today's Everest climbers relate to the mountain through a broader cultural lens, and not a mountaineering one. This lens is one of artificially manufactured adventure, where the focus is on ensuring success via the path of most certainty, and avoiding uncertainty and unknowns at any cost.

Most of today's traditional organisations can be viewed through a similar lens. As Lindblade describes of commercial mountaineering teams, 'within this fixed expedition style and structure, the individual can pass on the physical and emotional responsibility to the overall structure of the expedition'. As with expedition-style mountaineering, the traditional organisational structure is paranoid about uncertainty and attempts to cure its paranoia by building layers of bureaucracy that protect it and its people from uncertainty and ambiguity. It may ensure success in the short term, but it deprives them of the opportunity to truly develop important skills and gain experience—skills and experience that will serve them for the longer term of the new VUCA world.

Alpine-style organisations *will* on the other hand allow for the development of the appropriate skills and experience for the

VUCA world. They will not shelter their people from the realities of the outside world.

As Lindblade notes, while most aspects of our lives today are designed to ensure safety and certainty, the mountains offer uncertainty and an almost 'infinite potential for confronting and breaking barriers to personal freedom'. While it may be confronting, says Lindblade, it is what we don't know that can be of the most value to us as people. 'Strip away the elements of certainty', he says, 'and things get really interesting'.

Imagine what we could achieve if our organisations were inspired with this kind of attitude and mindset.

The traditional expedition-style approach to climbing a mountain is as outdated as the traditional, linear, hierarchical structure of the organisation. To understand why this is the case, we need to understand a bit more about this newer approach to climbing mountains.

The alpine-style ethos

As we have seen through the example of Whimp and Lindblade, alpine-style climbing is about moving light and fast to deftly climb the mountain and get back to base camp before the weather moves in. In direct contrast to expedition style, it involves fewer people, takes much less time, uses less energy and resources, and is generally structurally flat (there is no team hierarchy or designated leader).

At its core, alpine style is all about people letting go of their innate need to control an environment that is

naturally chaotic, uncertain and complex, and instead responding according to the natural ebb and flow of changing conditions.

While the last thing you would do when climbing expedition style is to give in to the elements, it's actually the first thing you do when climbing alpine style. If expedition style is about meeting and climbing the mountain on the climbers' terms, then alpine style is about meeting and climbing the mountain on its own terms.

In its most extreme form, alpine style is an incredibly committed way to climb. We saw that in the introduction with Ueli Steck climbing the Eiger unroped and without a partner. And the way in which Whimp and Lindblade climbed together was likewise incredibly committed.

But regardless of the limits to which you take alpine-style climbing, its key differentiator is that it sacrifices dependence on others (Sherpas and guides) and infrastructure (fixed ropes, tents, food) for the benefits of interdependence (working intimately with just a few other members) and lightness (taking only what is necessary).

Alpine-style climbing means the climber leaves the ground with nothing more than what they can carry on their back, enabling them to travel light and fast. In the dangerous alpine environment, speed is akin to safety. And so alpine style favours lightness and speed above all else.

Alpine style is an approach where the climbing of the mountain is simplified to its purest and most graceful form, where the climber, either climbing by themselves or with a very small team, is equal to the challenge of the natural state of the mountain; in other words, both climber and mountain are on an equal footing. Mark Twight, another leading proponent of pushing alpine style to its limits in the 1990s, notes that alpinists 'share a passion for climbing combined with the ability to exert their will and pay attention to both internal and external conditions'.

The alpinist is heavily reliant upon their own and their partner's skills and experience, which have been developed over a lifetime's commitment to the mountains. When you watch an alpinist in action, you are really only seeing the tip of the iceberg—many years (and, more often than not, decades) of skill development and apprenticeship lie beneath the surface. The alpinist has practised for 10 000 hours.

Why alpine style trumps expedition style

In his book *Finite and Infinite Games*, James Carse describes two ways in which we can look at our actions in life. Carse describes *finite* games as those that have a definite beginning and ending, and are bound by specific rules. Three- and four-year political terms are an example of finite games, as is the 9-to-5 desk job with only four weeks' annual leave.

Carse then goes on to describe another type of game, one that he calls *infinite*. Compared to finite games, infinite games do not have specific beginning or end points and, rather than having boundaries that constrain their players, they have horizons that move with the players.

Alpine style is the epitome of an infinite game.

Carse says the rules of a finite game *cannot* change, whereas the rules of an infinite game *must* change. A finite game is played for the purpose of winning, whereas the infinite game is played purely for the purpose of continuing the play. Finite players are those who win titles, whereas infinite players don't care about titles; finite players are those who play to become powerful, whereas infinite players just play with their existing natural strengths.

Most people today approach everything, whether climbing a mountain or running an organisation, as a finite game. Expedition style is all about identifying an outcome, and then doing whatever it takes to ensure it is won. It has a 'summit at all costs' mentality. Once the goal has been attained, once the climbers have returned to base camp, they can go home—the game has been won. Expedition style is extrinsically motivated, focussing only on the goal, leading to problems with goalodicy and increased exposure to the fallibilities of poor leadership.

Alpine style, on the other hand, is intrinsically motivated, focussing on the task at hand. The reward is learning from the journey as a whole, rather than just the moment of attaining the goal.

In the new world order we will need to move *light* and *fast*. So where do we start? To begin with, we'll need to know exactly what our current approach to the VUCA world is—is it expedition style or is it alpine? The next chapter will show us how to identify it.

A special warning: always be alert for the expedition-style organisation wearing alpinists' clothing!

CHAPTER 8

Making the transformation

> In this chapter, take your organisation from expedition style to alpine style by:
> - examining the traits of expedition style versus alpine style
> - using the Transformation Model to take your organisation from reactive to interdependent.

There is no doubt that if you look to the business world for a company using alpine-style principles, Uber is your go-to success story. They have ripped through the traditional public transport landscape like no other, and in doing so they have created a $50 billion company. Uber has bridged the gap and made the transition to alpine style; the taxi industry on the other hand has not. That industry is stuck in a place of reactivity and dependence upon the old way of doing things. Its time is coming to an end.

Here is a question for you, though: Who is the Uber of Uber? Who does Uber look to as an exemplar of working light and fast?

The answer is an Australian company that traded up 650 per cent in the first three months of its initial public offering. Like Uber, it is an app, and like Uber, it started from bare bones and a very simple idea. Also like Uber, it has turned the status quo of a long established sector on its head. It has seen how fear and uncertainty in the new world order can be harnessed, rather than shied away from.

The company and the app itself is called Reffind, and the concept is quite simple: using an easily downloadable smartphone app, Reffind integrates with an organisation's job opportunities, and employees are able to send available positions to their own contacts. The result? Employees get the 'finder's fee', companies hire only from known networks, and there is no middle man of recruitment consultancies. Already on board are companies including Coca-Cola, Qantas, AMP—and yes, Uber.

It's smart, quick, and easy to use—and it works. As CEO Jamie Pride says, 'Companies need our product ... We're a home-grown product, we're highly scalable and we have global applicability'.

It's an example of people, places and technology all being used to make a light and fast, alpine-style approach come to life.

As chapter 3 demonstrates, traditional old world organisations have a number of characteristics that serve to become liabilities in the new world. New world, alpine-style organisations do not have these traits. Table 8.1 shows the contrasting characteristics of the two styles.

Table 8.1: a comparison between the old and the new

Expedition style	Alpine style
hierarchical structure	networked/organic structure
reliant upon infrastructure	self-reliant
resilient and robust	adapts and improves (antifragile)
strategy focussed and backward looking	purpose focussed and forward looking
rigid and inflexible	adaptable and flexible
risk averse	risk embracing
controlling	gives up control
changes the external to suit the internal	changes the internal to suit the external
goal focussed	journey focussed
thinks linearly and sequentially	thinks nonlinearly, exponentially
metric driven, interested in quantity	experience driven, interested in quality
aims to be the best	aims to get better
led by alpha figure	comprises non-alpha figures
employs large numbers of people	has small teams
staff are disengaged and destructive	staff are inspired and destined
prefers the status quo	prefers VUCA
state of mind is dissonance and entropy	state of mind is engaged and in flow
plays a finite game	plays an infinite game
unaware, reactive and dependent	independent and interdependent

The terms in the last row of table 8.1 might be unfamiliar to you. This chapter explains what they mean.

When you cast your eyes down the left-hand column of table 8.1, what image springs to mind? I'm willing to put money on it being of a large, multinational commercial corporation that dominates the global marketplace. Perhaps you're thinking of one of the big oil giants, such as ExxonMobil or Chevron, or one of the diversified resources houses such as BHP Billiton or Rio Tinto.

There are literally thousands upon thousands of examples of large organisations like these around the world. Of course, not all of them are commercial ones either: for example, the US Department of Defense is the largest employer in the world, with 700 000 civilian workers and more than 2 million active duty employees.

However, regardless of the type of services provided by these organisations, they are for the most part similar in their nature and exhibit the attributes and traits identified in the left-hand column of table 8.1. And these thousands upon thousands of organisations are in danger of not surviving the VUCA storm. These large organisations have been put on notice. Transition to a new way of doing things, or die.

The Transformation Model

The Transformation Model illuminates the path. It shows us the five stages to becoming an alpine-style organisation. Inspired by psychologist Julian Rotter's locus of control (which suggests a spectrum on which people are located with regard to their beliefs about how they can control their own lives and the events that affect them), and DuPont's Bradley Curve (a model designed to help organisations develop world-class safety performance and culture), the Transformation Model can be applied at all levels: at the individual level, at the team level, and at the organisation-wide level (see figure 8.1).

Figure 8.1: the Transformation Model

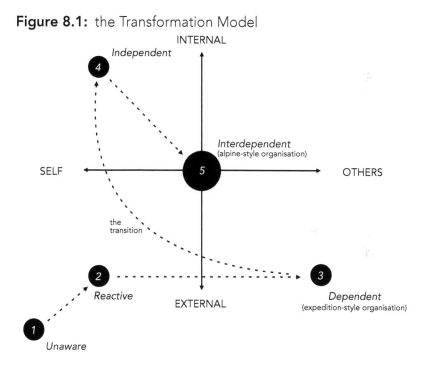

As you can see, the horizontal axis represents a spectrum: the left side represents a focus on the self, and the right side represents a focus on others. The vertical axis represents another spectrum: the top represents a focus on the internal environment, and the bottom represents a focus on the external environment.

Unaware

The first stage of the Transformation Model is *unaware*, where there is a lack of awareness of the self, others and the surrounding external environment. Accordingly, this stage cannot be placed on either axis and is located *off* the model. Table 8.2 shows the key attributes of the unaware state.

Table 8.2: unaware

Focus	Attention deficit—focus neither outwards nor inwards
Comfort level	Complacent
Engagement level	Disengaged
Decision-making role	Abdicates decision making
Resilience level	Fragile

Those at the unaware stage are like tourists passing through a foreign country, not even realising the language being spoken is different to what they speak at home.

Reactive

The next stage of the Transformation Model is *reactive*, where the focus is only on the self, and the ramifications of the external environment to the self. Accordingly, this stage is located in the bottom left quadrant of the model. Table 8.3 shows the key attributes of the reactive state.

Table 8.3: reactive

Focus	Attention in—they react to the external environment but their only concern is what it means for themselves
Comfort level	Uncomfortable
Engagement level	Actively disengaged and destructive
Decision-making role	Emotion and subconscious drive decision making
Resilience level	Fragile

Those at the reactive stage are like aspiring mountaineers, introduced to the mountains for the first time. They see danger and risk everywhere, and are likely to act in irrational and unpredictable ways, with their only concern being their own welfare. (This was very much me in the early days—the first time I tried to climb a big mountain, I cried. I think this may have happened the second and third times, too ...)

The reactive person or team is not only not committed to their work, but because they don't understand what is happening around them, they are prone to being destructive. Any and all blame for mistakes, or a job badly done or an incomplete task is always apportioned to the external environment, and to the team or organisation for which they work.

Those at the reactive stage may understand that things are changing, but have no understanding of how things are changing.

Dependent

The next stage of the Transformation Model is *dependent*, where the focus is still strongly on the external environment. However, there is a recognition that others will be able to assist by providing guidance, reassurance and comfort. As such, the focus becomes less on the self and more on what others can do for that self. Accordingly, this stage is located in the bottom right quadrant of the model. Table 8.4 shows the key attributes of the dependent state.

Table 8.4: dependent

Focus	Attention out—they react to the external environment and recognise that others may be able to help
Comfort level	Accepting—help is at hand
Engagement level	Engaged
Decision-making role	Mostly abdicate decision making; if decision making is required, emotion and subconscious drive it
Resilience level	Resilient and robust—because they have others they can depend upon

The classic dependent individual is the mountaineer joining a commercial expedition to the Himalaya. Although they may see danger and risk all around, they are less likely to act in irrational and unpredictable ways because they have a sense of security provided by the expedition's support structure (e.g. Sherpas, guides, fixed ropes, pre-established camps, prepared food).

It is at this stage that we find the traditional, linear, hierarchical organisation. If the desire is to transition to the light and fast alpine-style approach, this is where the transition starts.

Independent

The fourth stage is the *independent* stage, where the focus reverts to the self. A seismic shift has occurred here. This is where self-reliance and responsibility begin to form and take root. An understanding begins to form that the outside world cannot be controlled, and instead it is up to the individual to choose how to respond and adapt to the external world, which will determine their own success. Their attention is thus initially inwards. Accordingly, this stage is located in the top left of the model. Table 8.5 shows the key attributes of the independent state.

Table 8.5: independent

Focus	Attention in, then out—they understand that it is up to the individual to choose how to respond and adapt to the external world
Comfort level	Comfortable—they operate in a state of flow
Engagement level	Inspired
Decision-making role	Rational, emotional and subconscious drive decision making (full spectrum)
Resilience level	Antifragile

The classic example of the independent stage is Ueli Steck soloing the North Face of the Eiger. Everything that Steck did on the North Face exemplified these attributes of the independent.

Interdependent

The fifth and final stage is the *interdependent* stage, where the focus is now towards collaborating with others who have also reached this level. The understanding formed at the independent stage is now consolidated and is the fundamental tenet upon which the interdependent team functions. The attention of the interdependent is both in *and* out, at the same time. They are always keeping a check on themselves, their team members, and the surrounding environment. Accordingly, this stage is located in the centre of the model. Table 8.6 shows the key attributes of the interdependent stage.

Table 8.6: interdependent

Focus	Attention in *and* out—they are always keeping a check on themselves, their team members, and the surrounding environment
Comfort level	Confident and curious—they operate in a state of flow
Engagement level	Destined
Decision-making role	Full-spectrum decision making
Resilience level	Antifragile

The classic example of the interdependent is the climbing partnership of Whimp and Lindblade discussed in chapter 7. Everything that they did together exemplified these attributes of the interdependent. From their feats on Thalay Sagar to their ascent of Jannu, they were the epitome of interdependence.

Those at the interdependent stage collaborate willingly and effectively to achieve their own personal goals, as well as those of the team, and those of the organisation for which they work.

Rather than the linear, hierarchical structure of the traditional organisation, the alpine-style organisation is decentralised and interdependent.

As the Transformation Model clearly shows, alpine style as a philosophy can only work within organisations whose people and culture have reached the independent and interdependent stages. Without these, you can only have an expedition-style organisation, and you will not be able to transition from the old world to the new world.

A special warning

Always be alert for the expedition-style organisation wearing alpinists' clothing! Many of our expedition-style organisations are starting to recognise the benefits of the alpine-style approach—and they want in. But they are not really prepared to do the hard work. You'll be able to recognise them from their sudden adoption of corporate spin such as 'agile' and 'innovative' into their organisational vocabulary.

A superficial makeover will not suffice: that kind of delusional and complacent attitude in the mountains will get you killed very quickly. The same thing will happen for these organisations; and besides, the workers of today are savvy enough to spot stuff like that from a mile way. And they won't buy it.

Remember, an open-plan office complete with brightly coloured sofas and an in-house coffee shop does not an alpine-style organisation make!

You'll have to go much deeper than that, and you'll have to work much harder at it. How? That's what part III reveals: how in using the Alpine Style Model we bridge the gap from old world to new and create the truly alpine-style organisation.

The Alpine Style Model

Just like the expedition-style organisation parading in alpinists' clothing, simply looking the part is not enough.

CHAPTER 9

Three skills

> Taking yourself, your team and your organisation to the next level in a VUCA world requires some skills. This chapter is about:
> - **the Alpine Style Model**
> - **the sensemaking process**
> - **learning how to engage in full-spectrum decision making**
> - **making teams critical.**

While the aim of climbing a mountain in alpine style is to move light and fast with minimal equipment, there is some very specialist gear the alpinist relies upon to make it off the mountain alive. From lightweight technical ice tools made from futuristic compounds through to mountaineering boots containing Kevlar and thermo-reflective aluminium, alpinists' lives depend on their equipment.

Today anyone can jump online and kit themselves out with the latest gear. Just like the expedition-style organisation parading in alpinists clothing, though, simply looking the part is not enough.

In order to bridge the gap and transition our organisations beyond the unaware, reactive and dependent stages, and to move from an expedition- to alpine-style approach, there are three skills we need to learn, three insights that we need to have about ourselves, and three character traits that we need to possess. These are illustrated in figure 9.1. It's only once we have mastered all nine of these components that we will be able to reach independence and interdependence and create an alpine-style organisation.

Figure 9.1: the Alpine Style Model

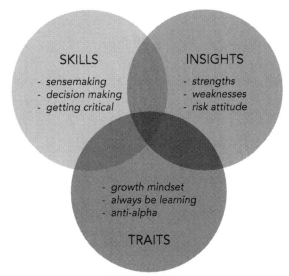

These nine components need to be embraced at all levels: the individual, the team and the organisation. They are what the alpine-style organisation lives and breathes.

So let's get into it. The first of these three skills is known as *sensemaking*.

Sensemaking

Danish philosopher Soren Kierkegaard once said that the problem with life is that it is most clearly understood *backwards*, but it must be lived *forwards*. So how do we live forwards when the world around us doesn't meet our expectations? The answer is very straightforward. We must learn to sensemake.

Sensemaking is the process where we develop plausible hypotheses of the unknown, test the hypotheses and then either keep them (if they are correct) or discard them (if they are not). Academic Karl Weick developed the concept in his book *Sensemaking in Organizations*, although smart mountaineers have been doing it since they first started climbing mountains more than 100 years ago, and alpinists have taken it to a new level.

In its simplest form, sensemaking is how we structure the unknown into something that is *more* known (in the VUCA world, it is difficult, if not impossible, to know something completely). Most importantly, it's a tool we employ *before* we start to act. Thus, sensemaking is an absolutely essential tool to have in the VUCA world.

Sensemaking is the process of devising a plausible understanding —let's say, for example, a map—of the changing environment, and then showing this map to other team members and testing its assumptions for validity, before further refining it, changing it or throwing it out, ready to start again with a new understanding and a new map.

Note the description of the map as being *plausible*, rather than *accurate*. In the old world, we had time to acquire the information needed to draw an accurate map, and the signals that we needed to pay attention to were clear. But in an uncertain and exponential world, we won't have enough time to collect all the information that is out there. Not only that, but in the new world, with its big data and overload of information, there will be so much 'noise' out there that it will be much harder to sort the meaningful information from the less meaningful. We will need to become expert at picking up the important signals, regardless of how weak they may be.

Although you might not have heard of the idea of sensemaking before, you probably do it all the time.

As you read this book, you are sensemaking. As you finish this very paragraph, you might pause for a moment, consider its main idea, observe how you understand it, and then integrate the idea into what you already know. If you are working with a group, you would then articulate the ideas to others.

Part of the problem with sensemaking is that it seems so darn *obvious*. 'You want to teach me how to make sense of things? Are you serious? I've been doing that since I was a kid!' But as with many things that we do as humans, just because we've been doing it forever doesn't mean that we are doing it to the best of our abilities.

I reckon it's possibly the most overlooked or misunderstood action in organisations today. It's common to see teams that are so overwhelmed by their daily workload that they seem to have either lost the ability to stop and observe how their landscape is changing, or they have lost the ability to articulate the changes to one another.

Have you ever sat down and read the instructions for your smartphone? Chances are you haven't; you just picked it up and started using it straight away. But you're possibly using less than 50 per cent of its capabilities. We do it all the time—we take things out of the box and start using them, never looking back. We have a bias for action, and for getting started on things straight away.

But that approach will no longer serve us if we want to thrive in the VUCA world. We need to go back to the box, get out the instructions, and sit down and read them. And make sure we actually understand them. You'll see this is something of a theme in this chapter: to begin with, we need to slow down *before* we can speed up.

If sensemaking is how we understand an uncertain world, it stands to reason that organisations that learn the art of sensemaking will have an unfair advantage in the VUCA world. They will be able to sense the nature of the game, its rules and how they are changing, as they play. And don't forget, this is an *infinite* game that we're playing.

In alpine-style organisations, your survival depends on sensemaking.

In your light and fast organisation, sensemaking should be happening all of the time. It can be used to look externally to learn about changing technology, changing markets, and changing competition, and it can be used internally, to look at your organisation's people, its politics and its culture.

In your new world organisation, everybody needs to be doing it. It is not just a process relegated to the organisation's senior management and board, as it traditionally has been with old world organisations; nor should it only be the responsibility of those serving at the organisation's interface with the external environment. (Besides, new world organisations don't have clearly defined interfaces between what is inside and what is outside the organisation. In the VUCA world, with collaboration, transparency and community, 'interfacing' is a constant.)

The irony of course, is that sensemaking is the activity we least feel like doing when we actually need it the most.

In the VUCA world, where cognitive dissonance, entropy and disengagement are the normal responses, it is our natural tendency to revert to what we know, and sensemaking it is not one of those things. We seek comfort in what we know to be true and to be certain—in the old world, that was reactivity and dependence. However, this leads us to rely on old habits and old ways of doing things, making us more rigid and less flexible. It's easy to see why sensemaking isn't something that comes naturally to expedition-style organisations.

One of the unintended but most valuable benefits of sensemaking in an organisation is that it helps build the working relationships between team members. Because it is both iterative and interactive, it is a social exercise, and because it happens in the early stages of the work process, it is a great way for a team to become familiar with each of its members. In many ways, sensemaking *is* team building. (If a team-building event doesn't include sensemaking, then it's not really team building, it's just socialising—more on this in the third skill described in this chapter.)

The process

So, what does the sensemaking process actually look like?

Dan Roam, one of the world's leading experts on visual thinking, describes his process in his book *The Back of a Napkin*. Although Roam's book was essentially produced to help people simply yet effectively illustrate business ideas in the boardroom environment, his key idea about the process of visual thinking forms a useful basis from which to learn the process of sensemaking.

According to Roam, there are four main steps to visual thinking:

1. looking
2. seeing
3. imagining
4. showing.

Just as with sensemaking, this process shouldn't come as a surprise to any of us; after all, we do it all the time. Even the simplest of tasks—such as crossing the road with your young child—requires it. Think about it: When I cross the road with my daughter, Lilly, I hold her hand, stand at the kerb and *look* both ways before crossing. If I *see* a car, I then *imagine* whether we have enough time to cross safely before the car arrives. If I decide there is, I then *show* Lilly, 'See, little one, it's safe to cross'—and then we're ready to move.

Of course, Roam misses the final step, which, while not so important in the boardroom, is critically important in the VUCA world—and that's *acting*.

So, sensemaking has five steps:

1. looking
2. seeing
3. imagining
4. showing
5. acting.

Let's very quickly explore each of these steps in more detail.

Looking

Roam describes looking as a semi-passive process of 'taking in' the information surrounding us, and gives examples of 'looking' questions:

- How far am I able to look?
- What are the limits of my vision?
- What do I instantly recognise, and what do I not?
- Is this what I expected to see?
- Do I intuitively know what I'm looking at?

Of course, this sounds pretty straightforward and obvious, but when you break it down, there's actually quite a lot going on when we 'look'. The first part to looking is the active, conscious part: it's where we consciously use our eyes to scan the environment surrounding us so as to be able to understand our context. We are seeking multiple sources of input: we are trying to gather as much information about our surroundings as we can. We have a thirst for data.

The second part to looking is where we unconsciously follow an order of looking, which is orientation, position, identification and then direction. For example, when you enter a crowded room, without realising it you are intuitively identifying:

- the orientation of the room and the people in it (are they the right way up?)
- where the people are in relation to the room, and to each other
- whether you recognise any of the people
- where there is movement in the room, and if it has any ramifications for you.

If you are unable to instantly perceive any of these things, it's likely that something is amiss.

Once we have looked and acquired all of the available information, we then start mentally laying it out, enabling us to make connections between the different items, to give it order, and allowing us to throw out what we don't need. Roam calls this 'practising visual triage'. This leaves us ready to start the second component of sensemaking: seeing.

Seeing

Seeing is the conscious process that occurs in our brain once we have looked. It is only once our brain receives and processes visual information (in terms of orientation, position, identification and direction) that we start to *see* things. (Although this seems strange, we don't actually *see* with our eyes; rather, we *look*. It is with our *brains* that we see.)

Seeing is the opposite of looking. Whereas looking is a process of exploring and gathering as much information as possible, seeing is a process of selecting and refining that information into things we can understand and recognise. That's why it's such a crucial component of the sensemaking process.

Imagining

The third step is *imagining*. Once you have looked at and identified what you are seeing, you need to think about why it is important. This is where your mind's eye comes to the fore, where you convert the visual images you are seeing into abstract concepts that you can manipulate in your brain. There are five ways of imagining what it is that you're seeing. Is it:

1. simple or is it complex
2. stable or is it changing
3. about quality or quantity
4. by itself or being compared with something else
5. ongoing or is it finite?

This process of imagination has two particular uses. Firstly, it forces you to explore your interpretation in greater detail. Secondly, it requires you to decide how you will show your interpretation to others, which is the next step.

Showing

The fourth step of the sensemaking process is showing the culmination of the previous three steps to your team members. This step is what makes sensemaking such a collaborative process. The reasons for doing this might be to inform them, to persuade them or to critique them—or perhaps all three.

Acting

The last step is about testing your assumptions by transitioning into action. This is when you start exploring the environment, taking your ideas and testing them at the edges of the external world. The initial steps of acting are always tentative: are the assumptions correct?

If we are confident, we then move: light and fast.

Mark Twight describes how alpinists get ready for the final stage of sensemaking on the mountains: 'They make seemingly random tentative probes, testing the mountain's weakness, before launching an all-out push.'

So how do we decide whether or not to launch the 'all-out push'? This leads us to the second skill we need to develop to become an alpine-style organisation—the skill of full-spectrum decision making.

Decision making

The great paradox of the VUCA world—remembering that the perfect storm of people, places and technology is largely of our own making—is that humans are not naturally equipped with the cognitive ability required to deal with the challenges of uncertainty and complexity. In chapter 3 we learned that cognitive dissonance, entropy and disengagement are the normal reactions to the VUCA world. And the quality of the decisions made by a person experiencing such mental malaise will be compromised.

You might think that in an old world organisation this wouldn't be such a problem, because the levels of dependence always ensured decision making was sent up the chain to the top of the hierarchy. That, however, is a fallacy: someone will still have to make the decision, and the rate at which decisions will need to be made in the new world order means that a single or limited number of decision makers will be overwhelmed very quickly. Not to mention of course that the person responsible for making the decisions is human too, and will also be experiencing their own dissonance, entropy and disengagement.

When we are in a state least suited to doing so, we are required to make increasingly difficult and complex decisions, and more of them. In the new world, we no longer have the luxury of time or the right amount of information (we will either have not enough, or way too much) to make decisions.

Imagine yourself in a complex and highly volatile environment. Ambiguity and uncertainty is everywhere. And you need to make a decision about what to do. The information you are receiving is voluminous, leading you to experience a sensation of overwhelm. Additionally, the information you are receiving is incongruent with your expectations. (Just as it was for most people on 9/11.) '*How* can this be happening?' you ask yourself.

At a time when you need to be making your best decisions, the human brain is least prepared to do so.

And so rather than doing what we have done in the past, which is to focus on the quality of the decision made (in other words, the outcome — i.e. 'Did we make the wrong or the right decision'), we need to focus on the quality of the decision-making process. There's a big difference between the two.

We need to develop independent and interdependent people capable of making decisions either by themselves or within their teams (as opposed to passing it up the chain of dependency).

When determining an appropriate course of action in an uncertain and ambiguous environment, everything else stems from the decisions that the individual and team make.

In order to understand how the individual and team become independent and interdependent, we need to be aware of what's actually happening behind the surface every time a decision is made. To understand this, we need to look at how the human brain operates. More specifically, we need to understand the complex thought processes that enable the individual and team to employ a high-quality decision-making process.

The neuroscience of decision making

The past decade has seen significant advances in neuroscience's understanding of the interplay between the brain's neocortex and limbic system, and the conscious and subconscious (or unconscious, depending on which term you prefer) workings of our mind. Much of this understanding has been popularised in a number of recent *New York Times* bestsellers, the best known of which is Nobel Prize–winner Daniel Kahneman's book *Thinking, Fast and Slow*. Although initially applied to economic theory, Kahneman's work has much scope for application to the challenges we face in the VUCA world. Indeed, Daniel Kahneman goes as far as to describe organisations as being 'essentially factories for making decisions'.

The basic tenet of Kahneman's work is that the human brain has two ways of thinking: fast and slow. Fast thinking is quick, intuitive (it happens at the subconscious level) and often emotional. Slow thinking, on the other hand, is steady, deliberate and rational. Kahneman's key idea is that all of our thinking falls into one of these two categories.

Fast thinking is energy efficient, but sometimes unreliable and often prone to systematic errors known as biases, or heuristics, and these can lead to a reduction in the quality of our decision-making process. Examples of fast thinking include the following:

- completing the phrase 'salt and...'
- whistling a tune while you are walking
- answering the maths problem: 1 + 1 = ?

Using next to no mental energy, your brain was able to provide you instantly with the answers (or in the case of the whistling, you didn't have to think about the tune you were whistling). Kahneman refers to fast thinking as operating 'automatically and quickly, with little or no effort and no sense of voluntary control'.

Slow thinking, on the other hand, uses a lot of energy — meaning the brain is reluctant to use it unless it's absolutely necessary — but it is very good at solving complex problems. Indeed, as you are reading this paragraph, trying to understand the difference between the two speeds of thinking, you are using slow thinking.

Slow and fast thinking do not always operate independently of one another.

Indeed, fast thinking is continuously generating suggestions (e.g. impressions, intuitions, intentions and feelings) for the slow thinking to consider and confirm. In the old, pre-VUCA world, when everything happened as we expected it to, the slow thinking simply adopted the suggestions of the fast thinking, with very little or no modification (and hence, limited energy expenditure).

In the new VUCA world, however, our fast thinking is continually running into difficulty, because not everything is happening as we expect it to. We are required to call on our slow thinking with much greater frequency until we adapt to this new VUCA paradigm.

Time and time again, our slow thinking will be activated when events are detected that are inconsistent with the model of the pre-VUCA world that our fast thinking has previously maintained. In that old world, people don't decapitate others on camera and post it on the internet, commercial airliners don't simply disappear off the face of the earth or get shot out of the sky by Ukrainian separatists, and companies don't spring up and grow to market valuations of $19 billion overnight.

So, what to do?

In short, the answer is we need to slow down before we can speed up. Just as Ueli Steck had been climbing for more than a decade before he set a speed record on the North Face of the Eiger, we need to understand and learn about ourselves and how we can improve the decision-making process.

Full-spectrum decision making

We need to be aware of where our rational, emotional and subconscious thinking sit in relation to the spectrum of fast and slow thinking. Once we are able to do this, and deliberately slow down or speed up our thinking as is required, we have mastered full-spectrum decision making. Figure 9.2 illustrates how they all come together.

Figure 9.2: full-spectrum decision making

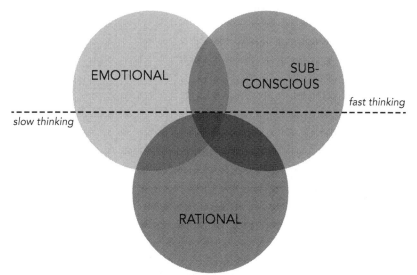

Have you ever been faced with a stressful situation and heard yourself, or someone else, say, 'Okay, just calm down and think about this rationally'? If you believe what you hear in the workplace then you'd be forgiven for believing that rational thinking is the only type of thinking that is important. Rational thinking is deliberate and steady—classic slow thinking.

Yet, to ignore the emotional and subconscious components of thinking when making decisions would be foolhardy especially in the VUCA world.

Emotional thinking at its most basic level seeks either pleasure or pain and is generally not easily regulated. Subconscious thinking is even less regulated (it is subconscious, after all), but can be incredibly influential and distort the facts in the decision making process (these are the biases or heuristics we referred to earlier). In order to make full-spectrum decisions, whether as individuals or in teams, we need to become better at identifying what influence these two components of fast thinking are having on us.

Being aware of our emotional intelligence

Emotional thinking can sabotage both the individual and team decision-making process because emotions can often override logic, especially in volatile, uncertain and ambiguous environments.

Having awareness of your own emotional thinking is referred to as *emotional intelligence*, and is described in the work of Peter Salovey, John Mayer and Daniel Goleman. There are four stages to developing emotional intelligence:

1. *Recognising the emotion.* 'What is the emotion that I'm feeling? Is it anger? Is it frustration?'
2. *Understanding the emotion.* 'I know why I'm angry. John didn't do what he said he'd do.'
3. *Handling the emotion.* 'Well, John has just got back from a day of sick leave so I shouldn't be too hard on him.'
4. *Expressing the emotion.* 'John, I'm frustrated that you didn't get that job finished, but I do understand it couldn't be helped given your recent illness.'

If we can all understand the basic concept of emotional intelligence then we can learn to shift the emotional component of decision making from fast to slow thinking.

Being aware of our subconscious thinking

If emotional thinking can override logic and lead to poor quality decisions, then subconscious thinking can secretly influence logic and lead to disastrous outcomes.

As we have learned with regard to slow thinking, the brain tries to expend as little energy as possible when making decisions, and this means it has a preference for using shortcuts. But, as anyone who's ever spent much time in the mountains can attest, shortcuts often don't work. These shortcuts are the biases and heuristics that we referred to earlier. It is these shortcuts that are often responsible for contributing to poor decision making.

In mountaineering, the most classic bias is known as Summit Fever. This is where a climber may be close to the summit and decides to press on despite the evidence that it is too dangerous to continue. The climber, so focussed on their goal of reaching the top (remember 'goalodicy' from chapter 6), avoids the use of slow thinking, which would suggest they turn back, and instead listens to the subconscious bias that tells them that they are so close, and have invested so much, that they should continue to the top.

In business you may have come across this bias, just by a different name—it's the sunk cost bias.

There are a multitude of biases that affect the decision-making process of individuals and teams, but here are four common ones that you'll encounter repeatedly in the VUCA world:

1. *The availability bias.* The tendency to base decisions on immediate examples that come to mind, e.g. 'That plane crash is the third crash in that area this year! I'm not going to fly there now.'
2. *The confirmation bias.* The tendency to interpret information in a way that confirms one's preconceptions: 'I'm sure we don't need to worry about that small tech start-up. Has everyone forgotten the outcome of the dotcom crash?'
3. *The cautious shift.* The tendency for a group to make more conservative decisions than they otherwise would as individuals, e.g. 'Personally, I think we should try it, but if the rest of the group thinks we shouldn't, then I guess there's a reason why.'
4. *The association bias.* The tendency to associate one thing with another, even if they are not related: 'This year's results look really similar to the results from last year's work. I guess the same factors are at play.'

Again, if we can all understand the basic concept of biases and heuristics, and learn to identify the multitude of different subconscious biases that we are prone to, we will be able to shift the subconscious component of decision making from fast thinking to slow thinking. Combined with our ability to slow down and recognise the influence that our emotional thinking is having, this is the key to enabling individuals and teams to make full-spectrum decisions.

So, we've learned about the two most important skills that we must have when operating in the VUCA world. As standalone skills they are incredibly important, but when combined with a final skill their efficacy can be elevated enormously to new levels, giving you an unfair advantage over everyone else. What's the final skill, you ask? You might not expect it, but we need to get more critical of ourselves and of our team members. Why? Let's have a look.

Getting critical

In his excellent book *Zero to One*, PayPal cofounder Peter Thiel tells how in an earlier incarnation of his career at a New York law firm, he had noticed that despite the partners spending all day together, they had little to say to each other. This confounded Thiel, who found himself asking: 'Why work with a group of people who don't even like each other?' As Thiel says, 'if you can't count durable relationships among the fruits of your time at work, you haven't invested well—even in purely financial terms'.

And although PayPal (now owned by eBay) is a relatively new organisation, this line of thinking has its origins in the old world, where one of the key organisational mantras was that we should all get along. After all, we spend so much time at work with our colleagues, it makes sense that we enjoy each other's company. To assist with this notion, a new industry specialising in team building was born.

This industry focussed on helping organisations improve the interpersonal relationships and social interaction between employees. In a sense, it was about moving team members to the right end of a spectrum that moves from 'not getting along' to 'getting along', and up a spectrum from being critical of one another to not being critical. The notion of team building was often confused with team socialising. It was the work equivalent of Happy Families. It was all about creating harmony and removing discontent, with the core belief being that only a team working in social harmony could achieve good results.

The industry offered such 'classic products' as scavenger hunts, mini golf and even paintballing.

Of course, there is a problem with these manufactured attempts at social cohesion. Common responses of most employees to news of imminent team-building events often include, in the following order:

1. an involuntary shudder down the spine
2. the rolling of eyes
3. a sudden urge to call in sick for the day.

That's because most people see them as a waste of time. And for the most part, they *are* a waste of time. I am stunned to see the ubiquity of these forms of team building still in practice today. Good organisations spending good money on a wasted opportunity to really improve how a team of people can work together. This old world approach to team building has absolutely no relevance in today's VUCA world.

The problem with old world team building is that getting along and getting critical are seen as polar opposites: a team that gets along is seen as good, and a team that doesn't get along, or one in which members are critical of one another, is seen as bad.

But real teams in the new world order aren't necessarily the Brady Bunch of corporate.

Team social harmony doesn't equal effective team performance. Why? Because concentrating on making people happy means an inability to give good critical feedback and unbiased reporting, which is, as we have just learned, essential in the sensemaking and decision-making processes.

In the new world, team building should still be about getting people to get along but also, and more importantly, it should be about enabling us to question each other on our assumptions and beliefs.

Of course, this isn't an open invitation for open and critical attacks on team members; rather, we should be encouraged to have open, healthy discussion about the work we are doing together and, rather than criticising, we should be critiquing one another.

Both sensemaking and full-spectrum decision making are tools that can be employed to great effect by the individual, but their true potential in the VUCA world comes to the fore when the critiquing power of the entire team can be leveraged. That's when the sensemaking and decision-making processes reach the status of very high quality. And that can help lead us to success in the VUCA world.

But of course, these tools by themselves are not enough. It's all good to be armed with the latest equipment, and to know how to use it, but there's also some stuff that you'll need to know about yourself, your team, and your organisation—and that's what we're going to look at in the next chapter.

Many of the teams in today's old world organisations were created as a result of circumstance, or by default rather than by design. And this is a real problem.

CHAPTER 10

Three insights

We are on to the second element of the Alpine Style Model, examining the three insights we need to have, through:

- an examination of the strengths-based approach
- the importance of consciously designed teams
- appreciative inquiry as a tool for building on strengths
- understanding our weaknesses
- an awareness of our attitude towards risk.

As we previously identified, in order to bridge the gap and transition yourself, your team and your organisation to an alpine-style approach, in addition to the three skills (discussed in chapter 9), and the three character traits we must possess (that's chapter 11), there are three insights that we need to have about ourselves to help us on the path towards independence and interdependence and creating an alpine-style organisation.

Knowing your strengths

In the last chapter, we heard about Peter Thiel's thoughts on working with people you like. And in the new VUCA world, it quite literally pays to listen to a group of people with a track record which speaks for itself: the seven founders of PayPal. Sometimes referred to as the PayPal mafia, they went on to collaborate on other successful tech start-ups, including Tesla Motors, Space X, LinkedIn, YouTube, Yelp, Yammer and Palantir: each of these 'unicorns' are now valued at more than $1 billion. (Tech start-ups with valuations in excess of $1 billion are known colloquially in Silicon Valley as 'unicorns'.)

Thiel describes his hiring policy at PayPal as follows:

> if you were excited by the idea of creating a new digital currency to replace the US dollar, we wanted to talk to you; if not, you weren't the right fit.

Thiel's idea was quite simple: to promise his employees what other organisations could not—the opportunity to work to their strengths, on a unique problem, alongside great people. Most importantly, Thiel's description shows what it can be like when a team, or organisation for that matter, is created by a process of design.

Consciously designed teams

Many of the teams in today's old world organisations were created as a result of circumstance, or by default rather than by design. And this is a real problem, because retrofitting teams is much harder than designing them from the outset. Based on many years of trial and error I'm a huge believer in taking the 'team by design' approach. Fortunately it's easy to do that when climbing alpine style. (The opposite is true of expedition style where, much like old world organisations, your team is what it is and you can't really do anything about it.) If I'm planning a climbing trip, building the team by design is really important. Not only will you be spending anywhere from a few days to a few months living in a tent with your teammates, your lives will depend on one another. I've been on too many month-long expeditions with teams that didn't really gel (and consequently weren't enjoyable or safe) to get this wrong again.

Strengths-based teams

Building upon the idea of a team by design is the concept of a strengths-based approach—that is, a team built by design, consisting of people with specific strengths that will complement one another in getting the work done. These are teams of people in which only limited additional skill development is required. It's all about the sum being greater than the parts. A mantra to remember here is 'although individuals need not be well-rounded, teams should be'. As Matt Church, CEO of global consultancy ThoughtLeaders, says in his book *Amplifiers*:

Focus on talents and strengths of the individuals and you will be able to drive better collaboration. When we accept that we are imperfectly perfect, we can drive more effective team building.

Of course, to do this, every individual needs to know what their own strengths are (and weaknesses or vulnerabilities, as you will see in the following section). And only people who are unaware, reactive or dependent do not have this knowledge.

The key benefit of a considered, designed strengths-based approach to building a team is that the result is strong, independent individuals collaborating as interdependent members. A team that has not been designed and isn't strengths based is much more likely to be reactive and dependent upon the organisational structure in the VUCA landscape.

IDEO is currently *the* poster child for innovation and design companies, and is renowned for its strengths-based approach to building teams. CEO Tim Brown describes how they look for 'T-shaped' people: people who have a depth of skill in one particular area and then a broader capacity to collaborate and empathise with others.

As Brown says,

> Most companies have lots of people with different skills. The problem is, when you bring people together to work on the same problem, if all they have are those individual skills — if they are I-shaped — it's very hard for them to collaborate … The results are never spectacular but at best average.

Tom Rath is considered to be one of the world's experts on the strengths-based approach. In his book *StrengthsFinder 2.0*, he makes an extraordinarily simple observation about our society's inherently flawed approach to education, which from the moment you read it you know to be true:

> at its fundamentally flawed core, the aim of almost any learning program is to help us become who we are *not* … From the cradle to the cubicle, we devote more time to our shortcomings than to our strengths.

Did you just have an 'aha' moment? (Don't worry, you're not the only one. The world is finally waking up to this realisation.)

Rath goes on to suggest that overcoming our personal deficits has become part of the fabric of modern Western society, citing as examples numerous books, movies and folklore (and many 'motivational' speakers, I might add) that celebrate the underdog overcoming innumerable odds to miraculously triumph, *despite* their lack of innate natural talent. (Remember, this is not an alpine-style approach. The alpinist has done their 10 000 hours.)

Think about how many times in your workplace somebody has been congratulated for overcoming great odds to get a particular project finished on time, or for having fought valiantly to overcome numerous obstacles: perhaps they've even received an award or gift in recognition of their efforts. This is very much the way that expedition-style organisations operate—remember, they think linearly, are strategy focussed and goal-oriented.

But what about those highly competent people and teams who quietly, expertly go about their work without accolades? How often do they receive recognition? (Of course, it doesn't matter to them, because they don't seek the recognition. As with any alpinist, the enjoyment and challenge of the task is reward enough.)

It's not about the end-goal, but rather the process.

As the solution to our flawed approach to education, Rath suggests the maxim drilled into us that 'you can be anything you want to be, if you just try hard enough' is perhaps misguided. Rather, he suggests, 'we cannot be anything we want to be; but we *can* be a whole lot more of who we already are'.

In his follow-up book *Strengths-Based Leadership*, Rath says that 'if you spend your life trying to be good at everything, you will never be great at anything', and that society's implicit encouragement of well-roundedness encourages mediocrity.

The strengths-based approach is the basis for any alpine-style team and organisation. Gallup, whose work on engagement you are now familiar with from chapter 5, has also conducted research into the benefits of the strengths-based approach. Not surprisingly, there is a strong correlation between a strengths-based approach and high levels of engagement:

- People who use their strengths at work are six times more likely to be engaged in their job.
- Organisations that fail to focus on the individual's strengths have only a one in eleven likelihood of their employees being engaged in their work.
- When an organisation's leaders focus on the strengths of their employees, the likelihood of employees being engaged increases to three in four.

The make-up of teams in many old world organisations has occurred as a result of circumstances and chance, rather than by design. (You're no doubt familiar with the highly competent technical person who is promoted to a managerial role but fails due to lack of people skills.) In the old world, expedition-style organisations could carry these people. The structure of the organisation was robust enough to contain their mediocrity. However, in the new world this will not be the case. The pressure and cognitive dissonance caused by the uncertainty and complexity will cause these organisations to break down. The average or mediocre team will not be able to function when they are in a state of overwhelm and reactivity.

Appreciative inquiry

Complementary to the strengths-based approach is the idea of appreciative inquiry. British academics Duane West and Frank Stowell developed the concept in the early 1990s and describe it in this way:

> Appreciative Inquiry … starts with the belief that every organisation, and every person in that organisation, has positive aspects that can be built upon. It asks questions like 'What's working well?', 'What's good about what you are currently doing?'

As a tool, appreciative inquiry is an effective way to support the process of exploring an individual's domain of strength and expertise.

This is in contrast to the other model for improvement with which you're no doubt familiar, the *deficiency* model commonly known as 360-degree feedback. This tool is used to provide feedback to an individual from all directions and, as it relies on the traditional hierarchical structure to provide feedback from above and below, expedition-style organisations love it.

The real problem with it of course is that it further reinforces the idea that deficiencies need to be improved: in other words, it helps form the well-rounded individual, not the well-rounded team of individuals. (Not to mention that the deficiency model can be incredibly damaging to the individual's self-esteem, and can have a large impact on team dynamics.)

Knowing your weaknesses

Now that we have established how important an awareness of our strengths is, you might be thinking, 'Excellent; now I can ignore what I'm hopeless at doing!' Sadly, not quite. While your natural strengths should be the bench upon which you do your best work, having insight into your weakness and vulnerabilities can be one of the most powerful tools at your disposal in the VUCA world.

Showing remarkable insight for one of the original old world management gurus, the late Peter Drucker said: 'Developing your strengths does not mean ignoring your weaknesses. On the contrary, one is always conscious of them.' Former Gallup researcher and author of numerous books on strengths-based approaches Marcus Buckingham goes even further, suggesting that we are actually *frightened* of our weaknesses. Buckingham says that if you know someone's fear, you'll also know their needs—because we all have an innate need to fix our weaknesses.

And this leads us back to the expedition-style organisation, and in particular, people who have a tendency to become reactive when the surrounding environment is not to their liking. One of the main sources of their reactivity is the fear that Buckingham is talking about. Their fear is an expression of the dissonance and entropy that they are experiencing.

Using this example, it's easy to see how we can be guided to an incredible extent by the urge to fix things that we are not naturally good at doing—it's what Rath identifies as society's flawed approach to education. This is the reason that Drucker suggests we should always be conscious of our shortcomings:

not because weakness is a bad thing (after all, we are all flawed), but rather because we can be blinded by our feelings of inadequacy and they can lead us to become reactive and to make unnecessary, and sometimes hopeless, attempts to fix them.

In the world of expedition-style mountaineering, a very sad example of the blindness that feelings of inadequacy can cause is that of Mike Rheinberger, a 53-year-old Australian who died on Everest in 1994 — on his seventh attempt to reach the summit. Having been thwarted on so many occasions over the previous decade, it seems that on this final attempt he had decided that he would make the top *no matter what*; he had told others that he was prepared to bivouac (sleep outside) on the descent — bivouacking at 8000 metres is a nearly suicidal proposition — and that is exactly what happened.

Along with his highly skilled New Zealand guide Mark Whetu, Rheinberger finally summited Everest at around 7 pm on 26 May after an incredibly long and slow summit day. (Rheinberger ignored Whetu's pleas to turn around once it became apparent how slow they were moving.) Like bivouacking at extreme altitude, summiting Everest so late in the day is also considered to be suicidal. Given the late hour, they dug a snow hole 20 metres below the summit and spent the night at an altitude of 8830 metres — the highest bivouac ever.

At this extreme altitude, nearly 9 kilometers up in the earth's atmosphere, at the edge of the troposphere where oxygen levels are 25 per cent of those at sea level and night-time temperatures drop below –50 degrees Celsius, both climbers suffered. By the next morning only Whetu was alive and he made it back to high camp with severe frostbite to his toes (all ten toes were subsequently amputated). If you've ever seen the excellent documentary of that climb, *The Fatal Climb*, you will never forget it—it's both tragic and haunting.

Was it a weakness—perceived or otherwise—that drove Rheinberger to push on when the evidence suggested the outcome would prove fatal? While Christopher Kayes's notion of goalodicy was no doubt at play, could it be that Rheinberger was *so* driven to overcome his perceived weakness (that he didn't have the necessary skills required to climb Everest) that it eventually killed him?

You can start to see why it's so important that in addition to focussing on our strengths, we are *aware* of our weaknesses. Not because we want to eradicate them, but rather because a weakness can become a trap that lies in wait for us when we least expect it. And in the VUCA world, the things we least expect will happen time and time again.

Now that we've covered our strengths and we've covered our weaknesses, let's look at the last thing we need to know on our way towards becoming an alpinist: and that's an awareness of our tolerance of, or attitude towards risk.

Risk attitude

The final insight required, be it at the individual, team or organisational level, is an awareness of our attitude to risk. This is important because in a VUCA world, we will find ourselves encountering risk on a continually increasing basis.

But as boring as this may sound, we first need to understand what we mean by *risk*. We hear its use in the organisational context on an almost daily basis, almost to the extent that people zone out when the word comes up.

And who can blame them?

With organisations' tendency to overly bureaucratise everything in an attempt to protect themselves from uncertainty, we have become an incredibly risk-averse society with astonishingly over-engineered risk assessment and management procedures. In chapter 4 we covered Yves Morieux's thoughts on the problems with layers of unnecessary bureaucracy, and that is in part due to our aversion to all things volatile, uncertain, complex and ambiguous. And this presents a problem. Organisations *cannot* operate light and fast if they are weighed down by layers of risk-management policies.

Like the conversations we have about change, perhaps we need to change the way we talk in our organisations about risk.

Because as we will find out, risk is not just a negative concept. With risk comes incredible opportunity. And the new VUCA world brings with it incredible opportunity. You just need to be prepared for it. (Which is why you're reading this book, right?)

For starters, what do we mean when we talk about risk? To many people, especially those in expedition-style organisations, risk and danger are the same thing.

But that's not at all true. If something is dangerous, such as a loaded snow slope waiting to avalanche, or unsustainable debt levels, there is no way around the fact that it is dangerous. Sooner or later, when a human interacts with it, they will be negatively affected.

So in other words, danger is *fixed*: something is either dangerous or it is not. It can by definition only be one or the other. If it is dangerous then there will be a consequence.

Risk, on the other hand, is not fixed, and nor, by definition, is it certain. Because risk is based on human perception, it *cannot* be fixed. The situational risk of an event can change based on the nature and experience of the person perceiving that risk.

For example, you might think that an expedition to climb Mount Everest via the North Ridge is patently absurd, whereas I think that with a light and fast approach, a small but strengths-based team, high fitness levels and excellent acclimatisation, it's a relatively low-risk proposition (at least when compared to climbing it in a commercial expedition). On the other hand, you might feel entirely comfortable leading a team of underground drillers 2500 metres below the earth's surface, or perhaps speculating millions of dollars on currency volatility, but they are both undertakings that are way outside of my personal level of risk comfort.

So, your individual perception of risk will differ depending on your own personal experience and attitudes.

The reasons for these differences relate to what psychologist David Hillson and organisational change practitioner Ruth Murray-Webster refer to in their excellent book *Understanding and Managing Risk Attitude* as our attitude to risk.

Our previous example about climbing Everest versus underground mining and trading currencies was a description of just that: our different attitude towards doing different things, based on our own skill levels and life experience and willingness to embrace the uncertainty that each of those things entail.

Hillson and Murray-Webster suggest that the situational factors that contribute to every individual's attitude to uncertainty will differ based on the following:

- the level of relevant skill, experience and expertise
- the individual's perception of the likely probability and frequency of the event happening
- the closeness of the risk in time
- the individual's perceived amount of control over the situation
- the potential for direct consequences.

My attitudes to climbing Mount Everest, underground drilling and currency trading will be significantly different to yours because what seems certain and clear to me might seem uncertain and ambiguous to you, and vice versa.

So we can begin to understand why danger and risk are completely different things, and why risk can be viewed in a positive as well as a negative frame.

If we can allow ourselves to think of risk as volatility, uncertainty, complexity and ambiguity *that matters*, noting that things that matter can be both positive and negative, it takes away the purely negative frame and enables us to see the potential upside to VUCA.

Given that by definition there are many things in the VUCA world that are inherently risky (remembering that they can be positive as well as negative), it becomes crucial that we understand our attitude towards risk.

As we can see, although it is a spectrum, there are five attitudes that can be easily identified:

1. *Risk unaware.* People, teams and organisations are unaware of themselves and their VUCA surroundings.
2. *Risk averse.* VUCA causes significant discomfort among people, teams and organisations.
3. *Risk accepting.* People, teams and organisations are okay with uncertainty and ambiguity; they are not necessarily comfortable but they do accept the discomfort.
4. *Risk comfortable.* People, teams and organisations are comfortable with the risks VUCA presents.
5. *Risk seeking.* VUCA does not cause discomfort; rather people, teams and organisations are very comfortable and look forward to the opportunities present.

One of the important things to be aware of is that our risk attitudes are usually subconsciously adopted, which therefore makes them prone, just like our decisions, to sabotage from our emotions, biases and heuristics.

The only occasion when this isn't the case is when a conscious decision is made by the person or team to override their automatic response, just like we have learned to do with full-spectrum decision making as discussed in chapter 9.

In other words, this happens when a conscious decision is made to shift the risk attitude from the fast-thinking space to the slow-thinking space. So again, we see that we need to slow down before we speed up. However, having the ability to recognise—to be aware of—our risk attitude ensures that when you see the fast-moving opportunities of VUCA, you will be ready to grasp them. That's the benefit of moving light and fast, alpine style.

So we have covered the three skills and the three insights we need to transition to alpine style. Next chapter we'll tackle the three character traits that we need.

By putting yourself out there, making mistakes and being open about those mistakes, beautiful and powerful things happen.

CHAPTER 11

Three traits

> **In order to transition to alpine style, we need to have these three character traits:**
> - **the growth mindset**
> - **a commitment to learning**
> - **an anti-alpha approach.**

Okay, so we have learned about the three skills and the three insights. Now we are on to the three character traits that we must possess to complete the transition to an alpine-style organisation. The first of these is about having an open, or *growth*, mindset.

Growth mindset

In her classic 2006 book *Mindset: The New Psychology of Success*, psychologist Professor Carol Dweck made a case for the straightforward premise that the world's population is divided into two types of people: those who are open to learning, and those who are closed to it. Importantly, this notion is also applicable to teams and organisations. Dweck refers to these two categories of people as having either a growth mindset or a fixed mindset.

The key premise of a fixed mindset is the belief that the qualities (of a person, team or organisation) are unchangeable.

Whether it is intelligence, personality or knowledge, they believe that they are what they are and that they cannot be changed. Whatever the external environment throws at them, they are impervious to it. People with a fixed mindset are more likely to take failure personally, regardless of whether they played any role in the cause of the failure. They interpret setbacks as signs of failure, rejection and of their own inherent weakness. They are embarrassed about their weaknesses, and do what they can to hide them from others.

As you're reading this description, you're probably starting to see some consistency here with other traits of the reactive and dependent expedition style: rigidity, inflexibility and guardedness (and embarrassment) around weaknesses.

In direct contrast to the fixed mindset, the key trait of those with a growth mindset is that their qualities are changeable and able to be developed and improved. They identify with their own strengths and weaknesses and are open to improving on these, but only if they feel it will help them in a purposeful way (in other words, they are learning for themselves, not because others think they are deficient). Whatever the external environment throws at them, no matter how challenging it is, they are ready to see new opportunities and identify new ways of doing things. Those with growth mindsets understand that they can evolve. They understand that failure is not the end of the journey, but rather an opportunity for learning. Rather than being embarrassed about their weaknesses, they openly acknowledge their deficiencies.

Again, as you're reading this you'll recognise the similarity with other traits of the independent and interdependent alpine style: adaptability, flexibility and openness and transparency around weaknesses and vulnerabilities.

To illustrate the difference between these types of mindsets, Dweck cites the example of an interviewer asking people what they would do if they got a C+ on a midterm exam, followed by receiving a parking ticket. People with a fixed mindset found this accumulation of negative events as a sign that the universe was out to get them and that life was unfair to them. People with growth mindsets on the other hand acknowledged that they probably hadn't studied hard enough and would need to work harder in the future (and perhaps be more observant of the parking signs).

Dweck notes that people with fixed mindsets tend to react differently to praise than those with growth mindsets. Children praised for their intelligence have been found to be more likely to adopt fixed mindsets; once they have achieved once, they no longer feel the need to improve any further. They have a tendency to bask in their success and to overemphasise their strengths, in order to avoid revealing their weaknesses. On the other hand, children praised for their efforts, rather than their intelligence, were more likely to enjoy working on harder problems and were even more likely to have increased their intelligence.

Does any of this sound familiar? Traits of the fixed mindset: goal oriented, resting on past achievements and a little desire to improve any further. Basking in past success, reluctance to reveal weaknesses. Sounds pretty expedition style. Traits of the open mindset: journey (not goal) focussed and inherent enjoyment from the work itself. Open to learning and not afraid to display weaknesses. That's alpine style.

In a 2014 TED talk, Dweck noted that one study using brain scans of children found that those with a fixed mindset exhibited reduced electrical activity (an indicator of brain function) when faced with complex tasks, supporting the theory that people with fixed mindsets avoid complexity and uncertainty. Students with growth mindsets on the other hand showed *increased* neural activity when confronted with complexity and uncertainty: they relished the opportunity of being challenged.

Are you convinced yet about the benefits of having a growth mindset for the VUCA world?

Don't Be Good; Get Better

Another way to look at the development of the growth mindset of the alpinist comes from Dr Heidi Grant Halvorson, who suggests that rather than focussing on becoming the *best* at what we want to be, we simply focus on *getting better* at what we do. In her 2014 99U talk (99U is the flipped version of TED: while TED is about big ideas, 99U is about making big ideas happen), Halvorson talks about the traditional *Be Good* mindset: it is about proving yourself to others and to yourself by demonstrating your superior skills.

The alternative to this is the *Get Better* mindset in which, instead of demonstrating your existing skills, you focus on developing them. And instead of thinking about your performance relative to other people, you identify whether you are performing better compared to your old self: in other words, are you improving?

Countless studies performed by Halvorson present results that show that a Get Better mindset helps people:

- enjoy their work
- find their work more interesting
- think more deeply and invest more consideration in their work
- increase their creativity and engagement with their work
- build persistence when things go wrong.

All of which, of course, results in superior performance, and makes people superbly prepared for the challenges of the VUCA world. As Halvorson says, 'you may think you can't afford to focus on getting better…The science says you can't afford not to'.

Both Dweck and Halvorson identify one of the fundamental principles of the alpine-style approach, and its difference from expedition style. Whereas expedition style is about becoming the best and winning at all costs, alpine style is about getting better, and enjoying the learning that comes with the journey. It's the same concept that James Carse writes about, as discussed in chapter 7. Both approaches are games, but one is finite while the other is infinite.

Indeed, Dweck notes that while research has shown that having a growth mindset is a predictor of long-term success, the flip side is not necessarily true. Once you have achieved success, you may even become more prone to developing a fixed mindset: after all, if what you did led to success, why would you entertain any other way of doing it? This closed mindset is in some ways a subconscious bias: you believe that past success is a predictor of future success.

This attitude breeds complacency, and in the mountains it kills people. In the business world it kills organisations.

Clearly, a person with a fixed mindset is likely to be more reactive to the external world in the event that circumstances turn against them. Thus, it's easy to see why developing a growth mindset is one of the most important elements to bridging the gap to independence and interdependence. These two stages can only be achieved if a growth mindset is prevalent.

The good news is that growth mindsets can be developed in everyone, and according to Dweck the single most critical factor in moving from a fixed to a growth mindset is simply *being aware that the two different mindsets exist*. So now you've got no excuse.

Which is a good thing, because you'll need a growth mindset to embrace the next trait.

A commitment to learning

Having learned about the difference between fixed and growth mindsets, when you think about the traditional old world education system that most of us have passed through you'll begin to realise that it exhibits many of the traits of a fixed mindset. It's a very linear process that aims to make you *the best*, and it's ultimately focussed on an outcome (graduating high school so you can get a job or get into university, graduating university so you can get a job, completing an MBA so you can get a promotion). Failing an exam is seen as a sign of failure and weakness, and is to be kept hidden from others (especially your parents) at all costs.

This linear process starts from a broad base of subjects when we are younger but over time progressively narrows until most people finish with a very specific and often technical skill set. In addition to the narrow specialty of this technical skill set, the skill set has generally been learned through the lens of *how* and *what*: *how* to do what is being learned and *what* that looks like in detail. Very rarely is the lens of *why* used.

But as the world evolves, the question of *why* will be more important than the *how* and *what*. Knowing how to do something and what to do used to give people a competitive advantage, whereas in the VUCA world it is a prerequisite. With the ubiquity of Google and Wikipedia, holding information is irrelevant. It's how you make sense of that information, and how you act, that is important.

The traditional linear and finite model of education no longer serves society, and it certainly doesn't serve our organisations.

Even if adults in the workforce are given the chance to learn, note that it is called *adult education*, implying that education is primarily for non-adults. The phrase even seems to have a stigma associated with it, perhaps implying that if the adult was very good at education the first time around as a child, they wouldn't need to go back again. That type of thinking is as ridiculous as it is old and entirely outdated for the new VUCA world.

If we are a product of our education, it makes sense that we are prone to fixed mindsets. It also makes sense that the way we think about learning is a product of our education system. The end result? We think of education as something that stops once you've got a job. We see education as being a finite game.

And that's a problem. Because in the new world order, education *must* be seen as an infinite game. If it is not, then the finite game you are playing is already over. These days, by the time you graduate from a three- or four-year degree at an old world university, the stuff you have learned in the first half of your degree will be out of date.

Which means the solution is threefold.

Firstly, always be learning. Never stop. View education as an ongoing commitment to your and your organisation's survival in the VUCA world. It will be as necessary to your survival as breathing and drinking water.

Secondly, be clear on what you need to learn to succeed in the VUCA world, and make sure you're open to learning about yourself (which will help you with all of the three insights from chapter 10).

Thirdly, be open to learning from unconventional sources. Undoubtedly, one of the sweet spots for powerful and lasting learning is once you've made a mistake. One of the problems of old world organisations is that the fixed-mindset approach tends to discourage mistakes being made, or encourages hiding them from view. Almost all of the learnings I have gained throughout my mountaineering career have come from making mistakes and never making them again.

While neglecting to learn in the old world of stability might have been considered by some as being lazy, your and your organisation's existence was not at stake. In the new world, however, failing to see learning as a key ongoing process is not only stupid, it's suicidal.

It should also be pointed out that we can't afford to outsource our learning to others. There is currently a sub-set of consultants and specialists out there who refer to themselves as 'futurists'. You may have seen them speak at a conference, or perhaps you've read some of their work: they basically conduct research and envision what potential futures might look like. Some are much better than others. But regardless, until now, they have been seen as a quirky specialty. Not any more. Ironically, the futurist is in danger of becoming redundant. Because not only do we need to keep learning, but we all need to envision what our potential futures look like.

We all need to be futurists.

So we have learned about the need for a growth mindset, and we have learned about the need to always be learning. The final character trait that we must possess to complete the transition to independence and interdependence and to creating an alpine-style organisation is one you might not have been expecting. It's about being the *anti-alpha*. What, I hear you ask, is the anti-alpha? It's a trait that most of us have; we just need to know how to uncover it.

The anti-alpha

The old world belonged to the alpha. Most of our organisations did too.

Who is the alpha?

We all know of the typical alpha leader. Highly confident, self-assured, and often opinionated. Extremely goal oriented, with a fixed mindset. Outwardly unemotional, with a lack of tolerance for others who display emotion and vulnerability: they think that to do so is a weakness. Controlling, highly analytical and metric driven, with a preference for force over subtlety. Their communication style is very direct, and they have a strong bias for action. They are sometimes renowned for their chest-puffing and, other than a firm handshake, they eschew physical contact (unless it involves football, and then brief periods of hugging are allowed). They drive for success above all else—even if it means personal life and personal happiness fall by the wayside. They epitomise success in traditional business terms as an expedition-style leader.

Our organisations have a strong history of being led by alphas. According to an article in *Time* magazine entited 'Top 10 Worst Bosses', an example of this could be Al Dunlap (colloquially known as Chainsaw). This American executive was renowned for his obsession with financials, particularly at Scott Paper in the 1990s, where he sacked a third of the entire company's workforce. Dunlap put financials above anything else, but his later actions at Sunbeam, according to *Time*, are 'widely viewed to have crossed the lines of accounting norms'. He was let go from the company shortly after.

According to Kate Ludeman and Eddie Erlandson in their *Harvard Business Review* article 'Coaching the Alpha Male', about 70 per cent of all senior executives are alphas. The main reason for their dominance in organisations in the old world? It's because the traditional, hierarchical organisation has always relied on a dominant figure at the top, calling the shots. The organisational structure requires this. An expedition-style organisation requires this. A new world alpine-style organisation, however, does not.

On the transformation model, the alpha sits somewhere between the unaware and the independent stage, but their dominant nature means they will *never* be able to truly collaborate with others to reach the interdependent stage.

The openness and unpredictability of the new world order means that those who can give up a certain element of self-control, as opposed to those who fight to retain it completely, will succeed.

This might fly in the face of what you'd expect to hear. In the new world order, where VUCA runs rife, surely we will depend upon those natural leaders who can stand up and face the challenges head-on, with a stiff upper lip and a battle-ready stance?

Not so.

Because the new world belongs to the anti-alpha.

Embrace your inner anti-alpha

When I was about to embark on my own climb of Mount Everest, a good friend delivered to me a message containing a widely cited passage from Theodore Roosevelt's 1910 speech in Paris, often referred to as 'The Man in the Arena'. Its key sections read as follows:

> It is not the critic who counts … The credit belongs to the man who is actually in the arena, whose face is marred by dust and sweat and blood; who strives valiantly; who errs, who comes short again and again …

> Who at the best knows in the end the triumph of high achievement, and who at the worst, if he fails, at least fails while daring greatly, so that his place shall never be with those cold and timid souls who neither know victory nor defeat.

I wasn't climbing as part of a large commercial expedition, instead opting to climb the mountain with a small team of my Sherpa friends. Although strictly speaking we weren't climbing the mountain in alpine style, we were bringing the alpine-style ethos to the climb: with only five of us, generally operating in teams of two and three, we were small enough and fast enough to avoid the larger and slower commercial expeditions. It was a different approach, and one that many thought would bring us a lesser chance of summiting.

Roosevelt's words were to me both reassuring and inspiring at the same time. I was never what you would call much of an athlete; and I am certainly no alpha. Up until this point in time I had always seen that as a weakness. However, reading this passage—delivered by a man who was a great orator (and a keen reader, which I am proud to be)—was the key to unlocking a realisation.

By putting yourself out there, making mistakes and being open about those mistakes, beautiful and powerful things happen.

Expressing vulnerability, I realised, actually made me stronger. By being the man in the arena, coming short again and again (as I had done, on many occasions), I had learned to embrace my anti-alpha.

This is the position of the anti-alpha. This is the strength and the adaptability that characterises who the anti-alpha is. It explains why they are starting, and will continue, to succeed in the new VUCA world.

Social worker and vulnerability expert Dr Brené Brown starts her book *Daring Greatly* by also recounting Roosevelt's passage, and how, upon reading it for the first time, she realised that it encapsulated exactly what she had been studying for so long.

Brown defines vulnerability as 'uncertainty, risk, and emotional exposure', noting

> Our willingness to own and engage with our vulnerability determines the depth of our courage and the clarity of our purpose; the level to which we protect ourselves from being vulnerable is a measure of our fear and disconnection.

In a world of volatility and uncertainty, where unexpected and sometimes violent things happen, we will all be increasingly exposed to these events and tested, time and time again. That resilient and robust exterior of the alpha might protect them, but it won't allow them to adapt. Like the old world organisations, they will be left behind. The anti-alpha, on the other hand, embraces vulnerability and doubt, because they allow us to adapt.

There we have it. The nine steps that comprise the Alpine Style Model. Can we go and climb a mountain now, or start transforming our organisation?

Not yet—there is one more thing to learn.

As the perfect storm arrives on our shores, *you* can be the person, or the organisation, in which people have faith.

CHAPTER 12

Pulling it all together

There are three final components required for the light and fast approach to the VUCA world. And the great news is, if you get the previous nine steps right, these final three happen by themselves — now *that's* alpine style. The final three components are:

- mission
- engagement
- antifragility.

Now that we have bridged the gap and learned how to transition to independence and interdependence, there are three final components that we must be aware of to enable us to venture out and into this new world order in a light and fast fashion. These final three components tie the earlier nine steps together and enable us, with lots and lots of practice, to become alpinists, advanced in the ways of moving light and fast.

So what are the final three components that tie up the Alpine Style Model? Figure 12.1 (overleaf) shows you.

Figure 12.1: the Alpine Style Model

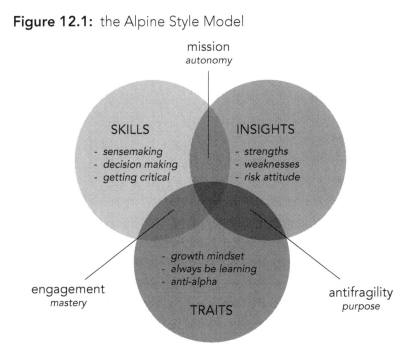

The three components are:

- *Mission.* This is about how we will launch projects in the new world.
- *Engagement.* This is about why we will want to do the work in the new world.
- *Antifragility.* This is about how we will adapt to the constantly changing ways of doing work in the new world.

In one final strange coincidence (yes, I know there have been a few so far), it just so happens that there is a strong correlation between these three components of the Alpine Style Model and the latest thinking and research on what makes work engaging and worth doing.

Daniel Pink summarises this latest thinking in his bestselling book *Drive: The Surprising Truth About What Motivates Us*. Arguing that the old 'carrot and stick' approach to workplace motivation of traditional organisations in the twentieth century is broken, Pink identifies three critical elements that contribute to creating work that is inherently motivating.

These elements are:

- autonomy
- mastery
- purpose.

Pink suggests that a combination of all three elements will provide the bedrock for all work in the twenty-first century.

Can you guess what the alignment with the Alpine Style Model looks like? Be prepared: you'll have to get your slow-thinking cap on.

They are:

- mission = autonomy
- engagement = mastery
- antifragility = purpose.

Not quite clear on the similarities? Not a problem: let's look into each of these final three components.

Mission

The mission is how we get stuff done in alpine-style organisations. It is where our skills and our insights combine. As we heard from veteran alpinist Mark Twight in chapter 9, alpinists test the route for weakness, and then launch an all-out mission. We go light, and we go fast. We take only what we will need, and nothing more. We don't sit around and waste time talking strategy and tactics—the time for that has passed.

We decide among ourselves—our own team—when we will start, which route we will take, and who will lead each pitch. We are not given orders by others as to how we should proceed. It is our choice: we have autonomy.

Pink describes autonomy as having a sense of personal choice about how we do our work: it's up to us to choose the best way to get it done. (And numerous studies confirm that when we have autonomy in our work we feel better about our lives and ourselves.) Autonomy is at the core of independence and interdependence, and of the alpine-style philosophy.

In the mountains, our missions mostly start in the middle of the night, anywhere from midnight to 4 am, sometimes even earlier, depending on the route. This is when the temperature is at its coldest and the ice at its most stable. It's called an *Alpine Start*. It's not particularly easy waking up and getting ready when it's so cold and dark, and both your excitement and nerves about the climb ahead will be elevated. But that's okay. This is the choice we've made—to climb light and fast, alpine style. And of course, the Alpine Start has its benefits—namely that the route will be safer, you'll be able to climb quicker, and you'll be back in camp before the rest of your competitors have even left their tents.

Engagement

Engagement is what keeps us focussed on a cold alpine climb, and it's what gets us turning up to work each day. It is where our skills and our traits combine. In chapter 5, we covered the problems with employee disengagement across the developed world. The great thing about the Alpine Style Model is that it takes care of this problem by itself. If you engage with the nine components then you'll find that people with any potential to sit below the 'engaged level' don't make it through the door in the first place. And if they do, they will not last there very long—it will simply be too fast and too uncomfortable for them.

The inherent strength in the Alpine Style Model is that it allows for everybody to work to their strengths, which in turn enables the pursuit of mastery. And mastery means that engagement will follow.

Why is this? You will recall our discussion in chapter 3 about psychologist Mihály Csikszentmihalyi's concept of entropy. Csíkszentmihályi describes the opposite of entropy as being optimal experience, or *flow*, which is when people are

> so involved in an activity that nothing else seems to matter; the experience itself is so enjoyable that people will do it even at great cost, for the sheer sake of doing it.

Flow is essentially what mastery is—when you are challenged in the work that you are doing to the extent that you lose yourself in time—but not to the extent that you are overwhelmed and too challenged.

According to Pink, mastery requires three things:

1. a person to be able to view their abilities (preferably strengths) as improvable
2. a willingness to get uncomfortable
3. an acceptance that *true* mastery is not possible (in other words, the Get Better mindset we learned about in chapter 11).

All three of these requirements for the pursuit of mastery are built into the fabric of the Alpine Style Model.

The good news for organisations is that in the VUCA world, where uncertainty and complexity are everywhere, there will be ample opportunity for committed, inspired people who want to develop mastery, because that's what the new world demands.

Antifragility

In chapter 2, we learned about Nassim Nicholas Taleb's concept of Black Swan events, and in chapter 6 his solution for this new VUCA world: rather than working on becoming resilient and robust, we must become antifragile. Being antifragile enables us to adapt and improve as we respond to the changing environment around us. In the Alpine Style Model, antifragility is where traits and insights combine.

But how does this relate to purpose? The purpose for any of my climbing trips to the mountains is always the same, and it always has two parts: firstly, to come back home; secondly, to come back home as a better person. (Note the Get Better mindset in action right there.)

The mental visual that accompanies this purpose again has two parts:

1. Getting off the plane at my hometown airport, the gates opening to reveal my lovely wife and daughter.
2. How I might apply my new learnings to *get better* in my life, be it at home or in my work.

If I feel I have nailed both of these, I know that the time away from home has been well spent. Knowing this purpose always keeps me focussed on what matters, and helps me to improve in the face of hardship.

Following the Alpine Style Model, a team with a clear purpose is always going to be inspired and destined to achieve, and antifragile in the face of the uncertainty and discomfort of the new world.

Pink's book confirms the idea that we *all* need to find a deeper purpose in the work we do. Autonomy and mastery is great, says Pink, but it must connect to something bigger than ourselves to really be satisfying.

What does this mean for organisations in the new world? In one word, it means opportunity. An amazing opportunity to do good; to do more than just return money to shareholders.

As covered in chapter 4, old world organisations will often attempt to define their purpose via linear strategy, using very metric-focussed, prescriptive, rational and quantitative terminology. But this type of language has no place in an organisation's purpose.

As Daniel Pink suggests in another of his books, titled *A Whole New Mind*, the future of global business belongs to the 'right brainers', where creativity will become a competitive advantage to trump other commodities. Those with creativity will be better equipped to express an inspiring and effective purpose that feeds the organisation's antifragility.

Getting clear on the purpose of what your organisation stands for, and why your workers work for it, is perhaps the number one thing that any leader of an organisation in the new world needs to understand.

Light and fast

And there you have it. That's it.

The Alpine Style Model in its entirety, with just enough information to get you thinking and started on your way to transforming your life and your organisation to the light and fast, alpine-style approach.

A final reminder

So it's really important to remember this: you and your organisation are *not* the only ones experiencing the discomfort and dissonance of the VUCA world. *We all are*. Every one of us. And so as clichéd as this may sound, we are all in this together. That means you, your family, your friends, your team members, your contractors, your customers—your entire community—are all going through the same sense of discomfort.

And so having read this book, there now lie in front of you some incredible opportunities.

As the perfect storm arrives on our shores, you can be the person, or the team, or the organisation, in which people have faith; you can be the pillar of strength for everyone while the storm blows around us. *You* can become an example of calmness, and of confidence, for everyone else.

The alpinists' example

Alpine climbers very much understand the realties of the VUCA world. They understand it almost without thinking, because it's a world they've learned to live in. Their one constant, apart from change, is the need to be adaptable.

Think of this in organisational terms and you will always be an alpinist. You will always be able to move light and fast.

The world of mountaineering opened up to me a world of possibilities I could only dream of as a child. I feel incredibly lucky to have had the experiences I've had. (But of course, it wasn't luck that made it happen: it was adherence to the Alpine Style Model!)

Although I have been fortunate enough to climb among the world's highest mountains, I am happy to say that I am not a particularly skilled climber, and as I grow older my abilities seem to be lessened—but not my ambition. It is, after all, an infinite game.

As a young man I was always in awe of climbers who, without fuss, went out into the unknown and tested their limits at the edge of human existence. To me, this was the noblest pursuit of all.

There is so much to learn from alpinists such as Whimp, Lindblade and Steck (who incidentally set a *new* record for climbing the North Face of the Eiger of 2 hours and 22 minutes in November 2015) as we enter this strange new world.

In my mind, theirs are lives without regret, with a flame of desire and a quiet passion burning within.

Rather than accepting a life half-lived, they pushed far beyond their own boundaries to live full lives of exploration and learning. They light the way for the rest of us.

They have shown us how to deal with volatility and uncertainty and with complexity and ambiguity, and they have done so with style.

This book is both a dedication to all of those who have gone before, and to all of you, who now are about to follow in their footsteps.

I wish you all the best for the future. Here's to alpine style!

With thanks

My mum and dad, Jan and David Hollingworth, introduced to me the mountains for the first time when I was 18 years old. It was a *life-changing* trip. They passed their love for the mountains onto me, and for that I am forever indebted. Thanks also for giving all of us kids the freedom to do what we wanted with our lives, and for being supportive of our choices.

My wife Natalie Rosser and our daughter Lilly, together the three of us comprise our very own alpine-style team. Natalie you have taught me many things but none more important than the importance of *unwavering* love. Thanks for supporting me on this climb, all the while you were climbing your own PhD mountain. And Lilly, thanks little one for bringing such joy into our lives and approaching this big new world with such curiosity. You are my favourite little alpinist.

My friends and mentors Matt Church and Jason Fox, the cleverest people I know, it is an honour to acknowledge you both here. Thanks for the inspiration, guidance, empathy *and* accountability. A big thanks also to Peter Cook, Dermot Crowley, Lynne Cazaly, Gabrielle Dolan, Simon Waller and *all* of my friends and colleagues in the Thought Leaders community.

My light and fast team who worked with me on this book, including Lucy Raymond and Chris Shorten at Wiley, who both worked *tirelessly* behind the scenes to get it done. To Lucy in particular, thanks for being such a believer in this book from the outset. My editors Kelly Irving, Kate Stone and Allison Hiew, you were fantastic in nurturing the book and shining the light ahead when I was stuck in the darkness, and my practice manager Geraldine Montero, thanks for keeping the lights on when I was in the depths of the writing process.

Finally, to all of the wonderful people whose stories or work I have referred to in this book (and *especially* Andy Lindblade and Athol Whimp). One can only get better by standing on the shoulders of giants—thank you all.

This book is written in loving memory of two beautiful anti-alphas, my friends Ankaji Sherpa and Namygal Sherpa, who both lost their lives on Everest. They died being in the service of others.

We all miss you.

Index

Patrick
Hollingworth

Are you keen to learn Alpine Style?

This book was essentially written to get you thinking and to get you *questioning*—*how* is your world changing and how ready for this change are you and your organisation?

The foundation for your thinking and questioning has been laid.

The business landscape is changing dramatically, and although this change brings much discomfort, it also delivers *unprecedented* opportunity.

Many businesses today are talking about innovation and agility, but do they actually know what it looks like in an organisational context? (Remember, be alert for the expedition-style organisation wearing alpinists' clothing!)

There are no quick-fixes here.

However, if you are keen to learn more, you can of course go much deeper and get down to the *nitty-gritty* of what a light and fast organisation looks, sounds and feels like. And that's where I can help.

I'm based in Australia and travel internationally to help organisations learn alpine style to become light and fast. I do this using the ideas you've just read about, via keynote presentations, workshops, mentoring and consulting.

So if you think or feel just a little bit curious to find out more, please get in touch, at either:

www.patrickhollingworth.com or hello@patrickhollingworth.com

Thanks,
Patrick

P.S. Because the world is changing so quickly around us, I publish a fortnightly thought piece on all things light and fast and VUCA to keep you up to date. Check it out at www.patrickhollingworth.com/thanks (hint: because you've taken the time to read this book, there's an extra special message filmed just for you, from the top of a mountain!)

Connect
with WILEY ▶▶▶

WILEY

Browse and purchase the full range of Wiley publications on our official website.

www.wiley.com

Check out the Wiley blog for news, articles and information from Wiley and our authors.

www.wileybizaus.com

Join the conversation on Twitter and keep up to date on the latest news and events in business.

@WileyBizAus

Sign up for Wiley newsletters to learn about our latest publications, upcoming events and conferences, and discounts available to our customers.

www.wiley.com/email

Wiley titles are also produced in e-book formats. Available from all good retailers.

Learn more with practical advice from our experts

The Game Changer
Dr Jason Fox

How to Lead a Quest
Dr Jason Fox

Ignite
Gabrielle Dolan

Hooked
Gabrielle Dolan and Yamini Naidu

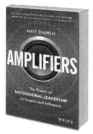

Amplifiers
Matt Church

Lead with Wisdom
Mark Strom

From Me to We
Janine Garner

Future Brain
Dr Jenny Brockis

Doing Good by Doing Good
Peter Baines

Available in print and e-book formats

WILEY